Crunch Point

Crunch Point

The 21 Secrets to Succeeding When It Matters Most

Brian Tracy

⊿MACOM

American Management Association

New York • Atlanta • Brussels • Chicago • Mexico City • San Francisco
Shanghai • Tokyo • Toronto • Washington, D.C.

Special discounts on bulk quantities of AMACOM books are
available to corporations, professional associations, and other
organizations. For details, contact Special Sales Department,
AMACOM, a division of American Management Association,
1601 Broadway, New York, NY 10019.
Tel.: 212-903-8316. Fax: 212-903-8083.
Website: www. amacombooks.org

This publication is designed to provide accurate and authoritative
information in regard to the subject matter covered. It is sold with the
understanding that the publisher is not engaged in rendering legal,
accounting, or other professional service. If legal advice or other expert
assistance is required, the services of a competent professional person
should be sought.

Library of Congress Cataloging-in-Publication Data

Tracy, Brian.
    Crunch point : the 21 secrets to succeeding when it matters most /
Brian Tracy.
        p.   cm.
    Includes index.
    ISBN-13: 978-0-8144-7371-9
    ISBN-10: 0-8144-7371-7
    1. Success in business.   2. Entrepreneurship.   I. Title.

HF5386.T81413   2007
658.4'09—dc22

                                                    2006015404

Printing number

10   9   8   7   6   5   4   3   2   1

To those brave men and women, champions of enterprise, builders of families and friendships, risk takers on the turbulent seas of life, who boldly go where no one has gone before, and never give up. You are the empire builders, the true movers and shakers of society upon whom we all depend. Long may you endure!

Contents

Crunch Point

Introduction

*"The obstacles you face are mental barriers that can be broken
by adopting a more positive approach."*
—CLARENCE BLASIER

Welcome to *Crunch Point*. No matter who you are or what you are doing, every person and organization experiences problems, difficulties, unexpected reversals, and crises that knock you off balance and must be dealt with right away.

It is estimated that every business has a crisis every two to three months that, if not handled quickly and effectively, can threaten the very survival of the enterprise. And each *person* has a crisis—personal, financial, family, or health—every two or three months that can knock you off center as well.

But when the going gets tough, the tough get going. It is only by facing the challenge of a crunch point that you demonstrate to yourself and others what you are really made of. As the Greek philosopher Epictetus once said, "Circumstances do not make the man; they merely reveal him to himself" (and to others as well).

Your crunch may come in the form of declining sales, reduced revenue, and low cash flow. You may lose a major customer or major sale. You can have unexpected costs or reversals where you lose your entire investment in some part of your business. People inside and outside of your company may turn out to be incompetent or dishonest. You may be lied to, or cheated and betrayed by your friends and colleagues. These sorts of things happen to everyone.

A crunch point may be triggered because a major customer goes broke without paying you, leaving you stranded financially. Your bank could cut off your line of credit. A major source of revenue from sales or borrowing could dry up. You could be unexpectedly and unfairly fired and find yourself out on the street. You could have personal problems with your family, finances, or health. In each case, you suddenly find yourself against the wall, in a crunch, with your financial or emotional success or survival in the balance.

Responding to Challenges

Between 1934 and 1961, the historian Arnold Toynbee wrote his twelve-volume series, *A Study of History*, in which he examined the rise and fall of twenty-six civilizations over 3,000 years. Much of what he discovered in the life cycle of those empires is applicable to the rise and fall of businesses, large and small, and to individuals. The lessons he discovered apply to your *personal* life as well.

Based on his research, Toynbee developed the Challenge-Response Theory of History. He found that every civilization began as a small tribe or group of people that was suddenly faced with a challenge from the outside, usually another hostile group of people. In business, the equivalent is usually aggressive competition and unexpected reversals in the marketplace.

Toynbee found that, in order to respond effectively to this external threat, the leader had to immediately reorganize the tribe or group if it was to survive. If he made the right decisions and took the right actions, the tribe would rise to the challenge, defeat the enemy, and in the process, grow and become stronger.

But in growing and becoming stronger, the tribe would trigger a confrontation with another, larger hostile force or tribe, thereby creating another challenge. As long as the leader and the tribe continued to rise to and overcome the inevitable challenges confronting them, they would continue to survive and grow. By continuing to grow through successfully rising to the unavoidable challenges, even a small tribe—like the Mongols, for example—eventually became a kingdom and then a large civilization, controlling vast lands, treasures, and people.

Your Own Personal Growth

What Toynbee found in the life cycle of civilizations is also applicable in your personal and business life. From the time you start in business, you will be confronted with problems, difficulties, temporary failures, and challenges of all kinds. They never end. No sooner will you solve one problem than you will be confronted with another, often larger and more complicated.

By their very nature, sudden challenges, problems, and crises come unbidden. They are unwanted, unexpected, and often serious in their implications. They also are unavoidable and inevitable. You can never stop them completely. The only part of the challenge-response equation that you can control is your *response*. All that you can determine is how you are going to respond to the inevitable ups and downs of business and personal life. Your response is under your control.

For this reason, your personal level of *response-ability* determines your survival, success, health, happiness, and prosperity. By responding effectively, you rise to the inevitable challenges you will face all your life. In learning to respond effectively, you will continue to grow in knowledge, experience, wisdom, and maturity. And you will eventually triumph.

There's a saying that "the North wind made the Vikings."

The philosopher Friedrich Nietzsche wrote, "What doesn't kill me makes me stronger."

Rising to the Challenge

The only way that you can realize your full potential, and become everything you are capable of becoming, is by dealing with crunch points effectively. The only way that you can achieve all your goals is by responding and reacting effectively to the inevitable crises of day-to-day life.

The key to performing at your best during the crunch times of your life is for you to focus single-mindedly on the *solutions* rather than the problems. The more you think about possible solutions, the more solutions will occur to you—and the better they will be. The more you think about solutions rather than problems, the more positive, focused, and creative you will become. The more you think in terms of specific actions you can take, the more in control you will be.

The most important quality of leadership is the ability to function well in a crisis. It can be said that *leadership is the ability to solve problems*, of all kinds, including huge problems that arise suddenly and unexpectedly.

Success, too, is the ability to solve problems. The most effective and respected people in every field are those who are the most capable of dealing with the problems that arise in that field.

The good news is that you have within you, right now, everything you need to deal with any problem or crisis you face in life. There is no problem that you cannot solve by applying your intelligence and creativity to finding the solution. There is no difficulty you cannot resolve by intense concentration. There is no obstacle that you cannot overcome or get around if you are determined and persistent enough.

There is a little poem that says:

> For every problem under the sun,
> there is a solution or there is none.
> If there is a solution, go and find it.
> If there isn't, never mind it.

Your job in crunch time is to rise to the challenge, perform effectively, and continue to move onward and upward. Now, let's move on to discuss twenty-one ways to perform at your best when you-know-what hits the fan.

"I don't think that there is any other quality so essential to success as the quality of perseverance. It overcomes almost everything, even nature."

—JOHN D. ROCKEFELLER

CHAPTER 1

Stay Calm

"He that would be superior to external influences must first become superior to his own passions."

—BENJAMIN DISRAELI

You have a wonderful brain with 100 billion cells, more powerful than any supercomputer ever built. Your mind can store libraries of information throughout your life, which you can access through your memory in a couple of seconds. You have all the intelligence and mental resources you will ever need to deal with any crunch you ever face.

In addition, your thoughts are extraordinarily powerful, with the ability to make you mad or glad, positive or negative, excited or calm. The thoughts you think determine the emotions that you experience. When you find yourself at a crunch point, when you experience a sudden setback or reversal, your very first job is to seize control of your thoughts and feelings to ensure that you perform at your best.

Assert Control Immediately

On the wall of one of my classrooms in school was a poster showing an extremely agitated man. It said, "When excited or in doubt, run in circles, scream, and shout." Unfortunately, this is what many people do in a crunch.

The natural tendency when things go wrong is to react or *overreact* in a negative way. You may become angry, upset, disappointed, or afraid. These stressful thoughts and negative emotions immediately start to shut down major parts of your brain, including your *neocortex*, the thinking part of your brain, which you use to analyze, assess, and solve problems and make decisions.

If you do not immediately and consciously assert mental and emotional control in crunch time, you will automatically resort to the fight-or-flight reaction. When things go wrong, you will want to either counterattack or retreat, neither of which may be the right strategy in a crisis situation.

Take a Deep Breath

me

The starting point of staying calm in a crisis is for you to refuse to react automatically and unthinkingly. Instead, take a deep breath to calm your mind and then think carefully about your next words and actions.

Imagine that everyone is watching. Imagine that this situation is a *test* to see what you are truly made of. See yourself as a leader; you set the tone for those who look up to you. Imagine that everyone is waiting to see how you will respond. Resolve to set a good example, to be a role model for others, to demonstrate the correct way to deal with a major problem, as if you were giving a lesson.

The primary source of negative emotions is frustrated expectations. You expected a thing to happen in a particular way and something altogether different has happened. You immediately respond in a negative way. This is quite normal. But you must resist this natural tendency.

Recognize the Two Biggest Enemies

The two major forms of negative emotions triggered by a crisis or setback are the fear of *failure* and the fear of *rejection*. Either of them can cause anger, depression, or paralysis. *I am*

| ~~You~~ experience the fear of failure when ~~you~~ are threatened with the loss of money, customers, position, or reputation, or in the extreme, the life or well-being of another person. This possibility of failure or loss, especially regarding money, triggers the emotions of anxiety, stress, or even panic.

The fear of rejection is closely associated with the fear of criticism or disapproval, or failing to measure up to the expectations of others. When something goes wrong, you may feel as if you are not capable or competent. You feel embarrassed and deficient. You lose face. Your ego is threatened. These reactions are normal and natural. All that matters, however, is how you deal with these fears.

Remember, *my* ~~your~~ *response* to the crisis is everything. This is the test. Instead of overreacting, take a deep breath, relax, and resolve to deal with the problem calmly and effectively.

Your Inner Dialogue Determines Your Emotions

Psychologist Martin Seligman has determined that your *explanatory style* largely determines your thoughts, emotions, and subsequent actions. Your explanatory style is defined as "the way you explain things to yourself."

Fully 95 percent of your emotions, positive or negative, are determined by the way you interpret the things that are happening around you, by the way you talk to yourself. If you interpret the unexpected setback in a constructive way, you will remain calm and in control.

Although your mind can contain thousands of thoughts, it can hold only one thought at a time, and you are always free to choose that thought at any given moment. Whatever thought you choose at the moment will determine whether you become angry and flustered or remain calm and collected.

Remember that most things in life don't work out, at least initially. Remind yourself that problems and difficulties are a normal and natural part of life. They are unavoidable. The only thing you can control is how you deal with them.

Keep yourself calm by refusing to *catastrophize*. Refuse to interpret the problem as overwhelmingly negative. Very few things are ever as bad as they seem initially. The four most important words for dealing with any crisis are these: "This too shall pass."

Study the Problem Before You Respond

Instead of overreacting, keep yourself calm by asking questions of the other people involved. Listen patiently to the answers. If there is a solution, your job is to find it by fully understanding what has happened before you respond.

Sometimes, talking over the problem with a spouse or trusted friend will help immensely to keep you calm and controlled. Go for a long walk and review the situation, examining it from every angle, seeking a possible solution. Remain optimistic, no matter what is going on. Look for something *good* in the problem or situation. Very often, what appears to be a major setback is an opportunity in disguise. The complete failure of a project, process, or business venture may be exactly what you need because it may compel you to channel your time and resources in another direction.

Seek the Valuable Lesson

No matter what happens, seek the valuable lesson in every difficulty and setback. Within every problem you face, there is *the seed of an equal or greater benefit or advantage*. When you discipline yourself to look for the good in the situation, and to seek the valuable lessons that the situation or crisis might contain, you automatically remain calm, positive, and optimistic. As a result, all the powers of your wonderful mind remain available to you to solve the problem or resolve the crisis.

When you face crunch time, take a few minutes to close your eyes, breath deeply, and visualize yourself as calm, confident, relaxed, and in complete control. Resolve to be positive and optimistic around other people. Speak kindly and courteously. Act as if you don't have a care in the world, and that whatever has happened, it is not really bothering you at all.

Crunch Point Actions

1.   Look into any problem or crisis you are facing for something good, a benefit of some kind. Often your biggest problem is an opportunity in disguise.

2.   Seek the valuable lesson in every setback or difficulty. Imagine that your problem has been sent to you at this time to teach you something you need to know to be more successful and happy in the future.

"Never give up then, for that is just the place and time that the tide will turn."

—HARRIET BEECHER STOWE

Be Confident in Your Abilities

"Courage is the price that life extracts for granting peace."

—AMELIA EARHART

A major setback can shake your confidence in yourself and your abilities. The natural reaction to an unexpected reversal of fortune is to feel stunned, shocked, and angry, as if you have just been punched in the emotional solar plexus. This response is normal and natural for all of us when we experience sudden reversals and disappointments.

No matter what happens, remind yourself that you are a thoroughly *good* person. You are a person of character, competence, and intelligence. No matter what has happened, you have the ability to rise to the challenge and deal with the situation.

Talk to yourself positively in order to rebuild your self-confidence. Say things like, "I like myself! I like myself! I like myself!"

You Can Do It!

Whenever something goes seriously wrong, you experience the fear of failure. You immediately feel this fear in the pit of your stomach. You may feel that you are not capable or competent. Sometimes, you feel like a loser. When things go wrong, in spite of your best efforts, you will often have feelings of self-doubt.

Fortunately, you can neutralize these negative feelings by saying firmly to yourself, "I can do it! I can do it! I can do it!"

Tell yourself that you can do anything that you put your mind to. Tell yourself that there is no problem that you cannot solve. Look upon solving the problem or resolving the crisis as a test of your character and intelligence. See it as a challenge, something that has been sent to help you to grow in knowledge and wisdom.

The Worry-Buster Formula

One of the very best ways to clear your mind and build your confidence in your ability to solve the problem is to quickly use the four-part worry-buster formula. Here it is:

1. Stop and identify the worst possible outcome of the problem or crisis. Be perfectly honest with yourself and others. Ask, "What is the worst thing that can happen in this situation?"

2. Resolve to accept the worst, whatever it is, should it occur. This action calms you down and clears your mind. Once you have mentally decided that you can live with the worst possible outcome, you will stop worrying.

3. Determine what you would do if the worst possible outcome occurred. What actions would you take?

4. Begin immediately to improve upon the worst possible outcome. Identify everything you could do to minimize the damage or reduce your losses. Focus all your time and attention on achieving the very best outcome you possibly can.

The Antidote to Worry

The only real antidote to worry is *purposeful action* in the direction of your goals. Instead of becoming upset or doubting yourself and your abilities, decide to take action, any action, to resolve the difficulty and get yourself through the crunch. Remind yourself that problems come not to obstruct, but to instruct.

Especially, don't take the setback or problem personally. In business, no matter how smart or experienced you are, 70 percent of your decisions will turn out to be wrong or disappointing in the fullness of time. Don't be surprised or upset when negative things happen to you. They happen to everyone who goes into business or accepts a position of responsibility in any organization. As they say, "Problems go with the territory."

Self-confidence comes from a feeling of forward motion toward your goals. Get so busy working on the solutions to your problems that you don't have time to worry about what has happened, especially things that you cannot change.

Crunch Point Actions

1. Take purposeful action immediately to deal with your problem. Do something. Do anything, but step forward boldly to take charge and minimize the damage.

2. Refuse to feel sorry for yourself or lash out at someone else. Problems are a normal and natural part of a busy life. Instead, accept responsibility for the situation and focus on the solution.

> "The universal line of distinction between the strong and the weak is that one persists, the other hesitates, falters, trifles, and at last collapses or 'caves in.'"
>
> **—EDWIN PERCY WHIPPLE**

Dare to Go Forward

"Courage is contagious. When a brave man takes a stand,
the spines of others are often stiffened."

—BILLY GRAHAM

When your business hits a crunch point, you must make the survival of your company your primary consideration. Desperate situations often require desperate measures. You must be prepared to do whatever is necessary to resolve the crisis and save the situation.

The most common quality of leaders throughout the ages is their quality of vision. Leaders have a clear, exciting vision of where they want to go and what they want to accomplish in the future. They articulate this vision clearly to the people around them. This vision then serves as a guide to motivate and inspire people to achieve at ever-higher levels. Vision is what separates leaders from followers.

The second most common quality of leaders is courage. Winston Churchill wrote that "courage is rightly considered the fore-most of the virtues, for upon it all others depend."

Everyone Is Afraid

The fact is that everyone is afraid. We all have fears of different kinds, small and large, hidden and exposed. Mark Twain said, "Courage is not lack of fear, but control of fear, mastery of fear." In crunch time, you must draw on your courage to make hard choices and decisions and to do the things necessary to ensure the survival and well-being of the people and the organization that depend on you.

The worst effect of the fear of failure is that it can cause paralysis. People go into a state of emotional shock, like a deer caught in the headlights. They freeze up. The fear of failure can cause even strong people to become indecisive and irresolute.

Do the Thing You Fear

Ralph Waldo Emerson once wrote, "If you would become a success, you must resolve to confront your fears. If you do the thing you fear, the death of fear is certain."

You develop courage in yourself by facing your fears and doing the things that you are most afraid to do. In business, the greatest fear (after the fears of firing someone or being fired, and financial loss or bankruptcy) is the fear of *confrontation*. Many people are afraid to make hard choices and deal with people in a clear, unequivocal, and straightforward way. They fear angry responses, argument, and conflict. This inability to confront people both inside and outside of the business can often be fatal to the enterprise.

Fortunately, courage can be developed by acting courageously. When you do something that you fear, you feel more courageous. In life, the courage *follows* the courageous behavior. You become courageous by acting courageously, even when you do not feel like it. Emerson also wrote, "Do the thing and you will have the power." Don't be afraid to make hard decisions, especially with regard to people and expenses.

Go into Crisis Mode

When your business experiences a sudden crisis, you must go into "crisis mode." You must act as though your business were on the verge of failure.

If you were threatened with bankruptcy, what actions or cutbacks would you make to save your business? Whatever you would be prepared to do to save your business sometime in the *future*, do it immediately. Don't delay.

Be aggressive about defending and protecting your business and your finances. Don't be afraid to discontinue, downsize, or eliminate any business activity. If necessary, don't hesitate to lay off or fire people who are either unnecessary or incompetent. The fear of firing an incompetent employee in a key position is a major reason for business failure.

The author Dorothea Brande once wrote that the most important advice she ever received was to "act as if it were impossible to fail, and it shall be."

The Two Parts of Courage

There are two parts of courage. The first is the courage to *launch*, to begin, to step out in faith with no guarantee of success. This is an essential part of courage that you can develop with practice. The second is the courage to *endure*, to persist in the face of disappointment and temporary failure.

Your job in business is to develop the courage to do whatever is necessary to fight the fire, solve the problem, and get through the crunch. This is the hallmark and the test of true leadership.

Crunch Point Actions

1. Identify some person, situation, or action that you fear; resolve to confront it immediately and get it behind you.

2. Whatever decisions you would make if your survival was at stake, make them now. As Shakespeare wrote, "Take action against a sea of troubles, and in so doing, end them."

"Some men give up their designs when they have almost reached the goal while others obtain a victory by exerting, at the last moment, more vigorous efforts than ever before"

—HERODOTUS

CHAPTER 4

Get the Facts

"The greatest test of courage is to bear defeat
without losing heart."

—ROBERT INGERSOLL

Perhaps the number-one reason for success in life is *clarity*—about who you are, what you want, and the details of the situation you are facing. The more and better information you have regarding the exact nature of the crunch that you are dealing with, the calmer you will be and the better the decisions you will make.

Jack Welch, the former president of General Electric and perhaps the top executive in the world in his time, said that the most important of all leadership principles is what he called the "Reality Principle." He defined the Reality Principle as "facing the world as it is, rather than as you wish it would be." Whenever Welch would go into a problem-solving meeting at General Electric, his first question would always be, "What's the reality?"

Facts Don't Lie

Harold Geneen, who built ITT into a 150-company international conglomerate, often said that the most critical element in solving problems and making good decisions in business was to "get the facts!"

You must get the real facts, the true facts, not the alleged facts, the assumed facts, the hoped-for facts, or the imagined facts. Get the real facts and make your decisions based on them. As Geneen explained, "Facts don't lie."

Whenever you face crunch time in your life or business, mentally call a time-out in the game and focus on getting all the information you can about the situation before you make a decision or overreact.

Ask the Right Questions

Ask key questions and listen carefully to the answers. Here are some that will help you get at the facts:

- What is the situation exactly?
- What has happened?
- How did it happen?
- When did it happen?
- Where did it happen?
- What are the facts?
- How do we know that these facts are accurate?
- Who was involved?
- Who is responsible for doing (or not doing) certain things?

The very act of asking questions and gathering facts keeps you calm and increases your courage and confidence. The more facts you have, the stronger and more capable you will feel about making good decisions to solve the problem and get through the crunch.

Remind yourself that "what cannot be cured must be endured." If something has happened, if it is a past event that cannot be changed, it becomes a fact. Never worry or become upset about a fact, which is something that you cannot change. Focus on what you can do, not on what you cannot do.

Dig Deeper for More Clarity

Especially during the fact-finding process, resist the temptation to become angry or to blame others for their mistakes and shortcomings. This is not the time or the place, if there ever is a right time or place for blaming. Focus instead on getting the facts, understanding the situation, and determining the specific actions you can take.

This means finding the answers to even more questions, again to achieve clarity. Two of the best questions you can ask in any crisis situation are, "What are we trying to do?" and "How are we trying to do it?"

Never assume that you have all the information, or that the information you have is correct. The more important a particular fact is to your decision making, the more essential it is that you check and double-check to be sure that it is true. Dig deeper by asking:

- What are our *assumptions* in this situation?
- What if our assumptions were wrong?
- If we were wrong with one of our major assumptions, what would that mean?
- What would we have to do differently?

Correlation vs. Causation

Finally, in achieving absolute clarity about your situation, do not confuse *correlation* with *causation*. The natural tendency of most people is to jump to conclusions too quickly. In many cases, when two events happen at the same time, or one after the other, people assume that one event is the cause of the other.

However, very often two events occur simultaneously or consecutively, but neither event has anything to do with the other event. Assuming causation between the two can lead to confusion and poor decision making. Don't let this happen to you.

In any crisis situation, when you experience a crunch point, imagine that you are your own management consultant, brought in to analyze the problem situation objectively. Act like a *problem detective,* asking questions without deciding in advance what needs to be done or not done. Get the facts. Facts don't lie. If you get enough facts and check them carefully, the proper solution and the right thing to do will gradually emerge.

Crunch Point Actions

1. Take a problem you are facing and imagine that you have been hired to analyze it thoroughly and make recommendations for solutions to your client. What questions would you ask before reaching any conclusions?

2. Determine the reality of the problem situation by getting all the relevant facts. Focus first on understanding what has happened before rushing to a conclusion.

"Before success comes in any man's life, he is likely to meet with much temporary defeat, and perhaps some failure. When defeat overtakes a man, the easiest and most logical thing to do is to quit. That is exactly what the majority of men do."

—NAPOLEON HILL

Take Control

"Courage is the ladder on which all the other virtues mount."
—CLARE BOOTHE LUCE

When things go wrong, when you experience sudden reversals and disappointments, your natural tendency will be to respond with negativity, fear, and anger. Whenever you feel hurt or threatened by loss or criticism, you react to protect yourself with the fight-or-flight response.

As a leader, your first job is to take firm control over your mind and emotions, and then to take control over the situation, in that order.

Leaders focus on the future, not the past. They focus on what can be done now to resolve the problem or improve the situation. They focus on what is under their control, their next decisions and actions. You must do the same.

Become a Turnaround Specialist

When a company gets into serious trouble, the board will often fire the existing president and bring in a turnaround specialist.

This specialist immediately takes complete control of the organization. He centralizes all decision making in his office. He takes control of all expenditures, right down to signing every check, so that he knows exactly what monies are going out of the company and to whom.

The turnaround specialist meets with every key person to get an assessment of the situation and recommendations for what should be done immediately to solve the crisis. He then acts boldly and often ruthlessly, making whatever hard decisions are required, including closing plants, selling off divisions, and laying off or firing hundreds or thousands of people. In other words, he does whatever is necessary to save the company.

Take 100 Percent Responsibility

To be your own turnaround specialist, to take complete control over your organization or business in a crisis, the first thing you must do is to accept 100 percent responsibility for yourself and for everything that happens from this minute forward. Leaders accept responsibility and take charge. Nonleaders avoid responsibility and pass things off onto others.

You especially must keep yourself positive and focused. You do this by reminding yourself and repeating these words: *"I am responsible! I am responsible! I am responsible!"*

Say to yourself, *"If it's to be, it's up to me."*

Above all, refuse to blame anyone for anything. Anger and negative emotions of all kinds are dependent upon blame for their very existence. As soon as you stop blaming other people for what has happened and take responsibility for the future, your negative emotions cease, your mind becomes calm and clear, and you begin to make better decisions.

Confront the Five Stages of Grief

The psychologist Elisabeth Kübler-Ross became famous writing about the various stages that a person goes through in dealing with the death of someone close. These stages are similar to what you go through when your business experiences a severe shock or setback. Understanding these five stages, and the emotions they trigger, can help you to bounce back from setbacks and disappointments faster than ever before.

The five stages of grief are denial, anger, blame, depression, and acceptance. These five stages are then followed by resurgence and taking control.

Your first reaction to a major setback will often be *denial*. You will be shocked and feel that this problem cannot be happening. It was not *supposed* to happen. It seriously disrupts your business and your life. Your first reaction will be to shut it out and hope that it is not true.

The second stage in dealing with a sudden setback is *anger*. Your natural tendency will be to lash out at people and organizations you feel are responsible for this financial or personal problem you are experiencing.

The third stage of dealing with death or disappointment is *blame*. In business, it is quite common for a witch-hunt to begin to determine exactly *who* is to blame and for what. People are called on the carpet, accused of incompetence or dishonesty, and often fired. This behavior satisfies the deep need that many people have to find someone guilty in some way whenever something goes wrong.

The fourth stage in dealing with death or disappointment is *depression*. The reality sets in that an unavoidable and irreparable setback has occurred. The damage has been done. Money has been lost. The feeling of depression is often accompanied by feelings of self-pity, of being a victim. You often feel let down, cheated, or betrayed by others. You feel sorry for yourself and wonder why something like this could happen to you.

The fifth stage of dealing with death or difficulties is *acceptance*. You finally reach the stage where you realize that the crisis has happened and that it is irreversible, like a broken dish or spilled milk. You come to terms with the loss and begin to look to the future.

Once you have reached acceptance in dealing with a major setback, you can move on to *resurgence*. This is where you take complete control of yourself and the situation and begin thinking about what you can do next to solve the problem and move forward.

How Fast Do You Recover?

Everyone goes through these stages—denial, anger, blame, depression, acceptance, and resurgence. The only question is, "How quickly?"

The mark of the mentally healthy person is a level of resilience in response to the inevitable ups and downs of modern life. As speaker Charlie Jones says, "It's not how far you fall, but how high you bounce that counts."

When you experience crunch time, when you have a major setback or difficulty, your job is to rise to the challenge, minimize the damage, and lead your organization into the future. Focus on what can be done rather than who is to blame. If someone dropped the ball, instead of being angry or punishing, treat the person with kindness and compassion.

Everyone Makes Mistakes

Recognize that everyone makes mistakes. Things go wrong all the time. Even the very best and most competent people do foolish things occasionally, as do you.

There is a famous story about Thomas J. Watson, Sr., the founder of IBM, who called a young vice president into his office after the vice president had just spent $10 million of the company's money developing a new product line that had failed.

The vice president came into Watson's office and said immediately, "I know that you are going to fire me for losing all of that money. I just want you to know that I am sorry, and I will leave without causing any problems."

Watson replied with these famous words: "Fire you? You must be kidding! I've just invested $10 million on your education. Now, let's talk about your next assignment."

Don't throw the baby out with the bathwater. Even the best of people, including you, make mistakes. When it happens, focus on damage control and what can be done in the future. Then, take a deep breath and let it go. That's the key to successfully resolving any business situation.

Crunch Point Actions

1.   Accept complete responsibility for the problem situation. Take command. Take charge. Get through the five stages of denial, anger, blame, depression, and acceptance as quickly as possible. Then get on with your resurgence.

2.   Refuse to blame anyone for anything. Accept that people make mistakes, and all mistakes cost money and emotion. Focus on the solution and what can be done now to solve the problem.

> "There is no failure except in no longer trying. There is no defeat from within, no insurmountable barriers, save our own inherent weakness of purpose."
>
> **—ELBERT HUBBARD**

Cut Your Losses

*"Courage is reckoned the greatest of all virtues, because
unless a man has that virtue, he has no security for
preserving any other."*

—SAMUEL JOHNSON

The most important quality for business success in the twenty-first century is flexibility. With the explosion in knowledge and technology, combined with the rapid growth of determined competition, both nationally and internationally, products, processes, services, markets, and customers are changing at a more rapid rate today than ever before. You have to be flexible in the face of this rapid and ceaseless change to maintain your mental health, much less to survive and thrive.

Charles Darwin wrote, "Survival goes not necessarily to the strongest or most intelligent, but to the species that adapts and adjusts most rapidly to changing circumstances."

Remember, 70 percent of your decisions in business will turn out to be wrong or disappointing over time. That means 70 percent of your products and services will not succeed in the market-place, or not succeed at the level that you had expected, and 70 percent of your staff will not turn out to produce the quality of work that you had hoped for. Even the best decisions you have made can be invalidated because the situation or circumstances will have changed in the meantime.

Knowing What You Know Now

Perhaps the most important tool that you can use to remain flex-ible and adaptable in turbulent times, and to deal with the inevi-table crunch points that will befall you, is what I call "zero-based thinking."

In zero-based thinking, you stop, stand back, and look at your business objectively, as though you were an outsider looking in. You ask this question: "Is there anything that I am doing today that, knowing what I now know, I wouldn't get into again if I was starting it up again today?"

Discipline yourself to ask and answer this question honestly on a regular basis. It takes tremendous courage to confront the reality of your current situation by asking the "Knowing what I now know . . ." question about everything you are doing.

Is there any product or service that, knowing what you now know, you would not offer or bring to the market if you had it to do over again today?

If there is, your next question must be, "How do I discontinue this product or service, and how fast?"

Management expert Peter Drucker calls this the process of "creative abandonment." You must be prepared to abandon any product or service that is draining time and resources away from the sale and delivery of more popular and profitable products and services.

A Question to Ask About Everything

Is there any activity or business process that, knowing what you know now, you wouldn't start up again today?

Is there any expense, method, or procedure in the operations of your business that, knowing what you now know, you wouldn't start again today?

Are there any people in your business whom you would not hire back again today, *knowing what you now know?* If they walked in today to apply for their current job, would you hire them for that job? Is there anyone in your business you would not promote, or assign or give a particular responsibility to, knowing what you now know?

Is there any relationship or situation in your personal life that, knowing what you now know, you wouldn't get into again today, if you could do it over?

If there is anything that you would not get into again today, knowing what you now know, you must move quickly to cut it off and get out of it as quickly as possible. The failure to ask and answer this question honestly can potentially lead to the downfall of the business.

Starting Again Across the Street

Another way to determine where you can cut your losses is to imagine that you arrived at work one morning only to find that your entire business had burned to the ground. Fortunately, your staff was safe and standing around in the parking lot watching the building as it was consumed in flames.

As it turns out, there are offices available across the street that you could move into immediately and restart your business. If this happened to you and you were starting your business over again today:

- What products or services would you immediately start producing for sale?
- What products or services would you *not* offer again today?
- What customers would you contact immediately?
- What business activities would you engage in first?

- What business activities, processes, investments, and expenses would you *not* get into again if you were starting over?

- Which of your staff members would you bring with you and who would you leave in the parking lot? Who are your most important people and who are the people you could do without?

If ever you would downsize, discontinue, or eliminate anything or anyone to save your business, you should do it *immediately*. Don't delay. Cut off all nonessential expenses and eliminate all nonessential activities. Get back to basics. Focus on the 20 percent of your products, services, and people that account for most of your results.

Your willingness to make the hard decisions necessary in a crisis, and to cut your losses sooner rather than later, largely determines your success or failure, both in the short term and in the long term.

Crunch Point Actions

1.   Apply zero-based thinking to every part of your business and your personal life. Is there anything you are doing today that you would not start up or get into again, knowing what you now know?

2.   Imagine that you could start your business or personal life over again today. What would you get into and what would you get out of? What would you start up and what would you let go of?

"Austere perseverance, harsh and continuous, rarely fails of its purpose, for its silent power grows irresistibly greater with time."

—JOHANN WOLFGANG VON GOETHE

CHAPTER 7

Manage the Crisis

*"To be courageous means to be afraid but to go a
little step forward anyway."*

—BEVERLY SMITH

In a fast-changing, turbulent, highly competitive business environment, you will have a crisis of some kind every two or three months. You also could have a financial crisis, a family crisis, a personal crisis, or a health crisis with the same frequency.

By definition, the crisis will be a *major* problem or setback that happens completely unexpectedly, is disruptive, and takes precedence over whatever else you are doing at the moment. A crisis forces you to go on *"Red Alert!"*

A crisis is a critical moment, a "testing time." Whatever you choose to do, or fail to do, can be extraordinarily important and have significant positive or negative consequences for the future of your business or your personal life.

Take Charge Immediately

When the crisis occurs, there are four things you should do immediately.

1. *Stop the bleeding.* Practice damage control. Put every possible limitation on losses. Preserve cash at all costs.
2. *Gather information.* Get the facts. Speak to the key people and find out exactly what you are dealing with.
3. *Solve the problem.* Discipline yourself to think only in terms of solutions, about what you can do immediately to minimize the damage and fix the problem.
4. *Become action-oriented.* Think in terms of your next step. Often any decision is better than no decision.

Remind yourself that you are up to the task. You can do it. You can find an answer and resolve this crisis. You have all the skills, intelligence, experience, and abilities that you need to handle this crisis effectively. Remember that there is always an answer, a solution of some kind, and your job is to find it. Often the solution is contained within the problem.

Practice Thinking Ahead

One of the key strategies for business and personal success is "crisis anticipation." This strategy is practiced by top people in every field—executives, managers, entrepreneurs, and leaders, especially military leaders.

You practice crisis anticipation by looking into the future three, six, nine, and twelve months ahead and asking, "What could happen to disrupt my business or personal life?" Of all the things that could happen, what are the *worst possible things* that could happen?

Refuse to play games with your own mind. Don't wish, hope, or pretend that certain things could never happen to you. This way of thinking could be disastrous, and needlessly so.

Develop an "If this happened, then what?" mentality. Even if there is only a small probability that something disastrous could occur, the superior thinker carefully considers all the possible consequences of that disaster occurring and prepares accordingly.

Develop a Contingency Plan

You need to have a contingency plan for possible emergencies and crises. What steps would you take if something went seriously wrong? What would you do *first*? What would you do *second*? How would you react?

Develop a scenario—a story line and a plan—describing how you would handle a negative situation, if it occurred. This is called "extrapolatory thinking" and is the hallmark of superior problem solvers. They look down the road into the future, imagine what could happen, and then come back to the present to plan well in advance of the possible occurrence.

J. Paul Getty, at one time the richest man in the world, was once asked how he thought about risk. He replied that when he entered into a business deal, the first thing he asked was, "What is the worst possible thing that can happen in this situation?" He then made every effort to guarantee that the worst possible outcome did not occur. You should do the same.

Prevent the Recurring Crisis

A crisis, by definition, is a once-only, unexpected, negative event. If there is a recurring crisis in your company or your life, one that repeats itself regularly, especially a cash crisis, then you are dealing with a deeper problem, usually incompetence or poor organization.

To ensure that the crisis does not repeat itself, after you have resolved that crisis for the first time, do a thorough debriefing on the problem. What exactly happened? How did it happen? What did we learn? What could we do to make sure it doesn't happen again?

According to Stanford University research into the top CEOs among the Fortune 1000 corporations, the single most important quality of the best leaders was their ability to deal with a crisis when it occurred. How you manage the inevitable crisis is the true measure of your level of wisdom and maturity. Your ability to anticipate a crisis, and to learn from it, is absolutely essential to your ability to deal with subsequent crises when they occur.

Crunch Point Actions

1.   Identify the three worst things that could happen in your business in the next year. What could you do today to minimize the damage from these crises?

2.   Identify the three worst things that could happen in your personal and family life, and then take steps to make sure they don't happen.

> "Our greatest glory is not in never failing, but in rising every time we fail."
>
> —CONFUCIUS

Communicate Constantly

"The best measure of courage is the fear that is overcome."

—NORMAN F. DIXON

Eighty-five percent of the problems in your business and personal life are going to be caused by your inability to communicate effectively with the important people around you. During a crunch point, you must keep the key people inside and outside of your business informed about what is going on. This action can make all the difference between success and failure.

Resolve to practice a "No Surprises!" policy with everyone. Surprises are seldom good. Nobody likes to hear bad news through the grapevine, especially if they feel that it is being kept from them for some reason.

People are highly emotional about both their money and their work. Most people react in a negative way to any threat of losing their money, for any reason. Employees feel threatened and become very emotional if they feel that their job or pay is threatened.

Deal Quickly with Money Matters

In many cases, crunch time in your company will be caused by a cash crunch, a dramatic shortfall of the money you need to run your business. In this case, you must move quickly to stop the bleeding and to comfort and reassure the people who'll be affected by these financial problems.

Sit your staff down and tell them the situation. Clearly and calmly, without exaggeration or excitement, explain exactly what has happened. Explain to your employees what you are doing to resolve the crisis and what each of their roles will be in helping your company to get through this period of difficulty.

Ask for their ideas and suggestions on ways to cut costs or to accelerate payments. Ask them if they have any ideas to help the business get through this crunch. You will be amazed at the quality of the suggestions that you get from your people if you invite them.

Bad News Travels Really Fast

The only thing faster than the speed of light is the speed at which a rumor about your business spreads, both internally and externally. No matter how much you try to keep something secret, the worst possible news will get to the worst person faster than a flash of summer lightning. I have had people at my seminars tell me casually about a cash crunch of a client on the other side of the country, which later turned out to be true. The speed at which people find and transmit this information is faster than the Internet.

When we were children, the rule was, "Beat the news home." In other words, don't allow news to get to the critical people in your business and financial life ahead of you. Be sure that you are the one who tells them first.

Adopt a Leadership Strategy

George Washington was able to keep his army together and eventually win the Revolutionary War by continually sitting his officers down in the middle of a crisis situation and asking for their advice. Invariably, the ideas and strategies that came out of those sessions led to actions and victories that ultimately determined the course of the war.

On the other hand, General Cornwallis, commander of the British troops, never entrusted his officers with any information. He kept all news to himself. He made his decisions in private. He would then emerge from his quarters and announce to his officers and to the army what they were going to do. By the end of the war, even though he had vastly superior forces at the beginning, he was defeated by a ragtag army that functioned on the basis of consensus and discussion. There is a lesson here for all of us.

Practice "No Surprises" in Financial Matters

If you have financial problems, practice the "No Surprises" principle with your bank, your suppliers, and each of your creditors. Tell them your situation before they find out indirectly. Whatever you do, do not hide your financial crisis or stonewall on the payment of your debts.

With your bank, go in person and sit down with your banker. Explain the situation that you are facing. Explain that it is temporary and that you have embarked on a plan of action to resolve your financial problems. Offer to pay "interest only" on your loans until you have turned your situation around.

What many businesspeople do not understand is that a "nonperforming loan" becomes a red flag and a major problem to the banker in charge of your account. He has no choice, under banking regulations, but to act immediately to protect the bank's assets by seizing your bank account or even foreclosing on the collateral that you have put up for the loan.

However, if you agree to pay interest only, the loan continues to be classified as active and triggers no consequences. Learning this little factor saved my financial life some years ago.

Be Honest and Straightforward

With your creditors, call or visit them personally and tell them your situation. Don't refuse to pay your bills, pay them late, or send them checks for which you have insufficient funds. Instead, explain your financial situation and offer to make monthly payments of smaller amounts until you get your financial situation under control.

Your suppliers and vendors are quite aware that their customers occasionally experience cash shortfalls. They are usually experienced businesspeople and, as a result, can be quite reasonable. But they like openness and honesty, not subterfuge and denial. If you tell them straightforwardly that you have financial problems and assure them that you will pay them in full as soon as you are back on your feet, they will usually relax and cut you all the slack you need.

Lead from the Front

Here is an important point. There are some things that you can *delegate* to others and some things that you must do *personally*. You are the commander in chief. When your business runs into financial trouble, it is you and only you who must personally deal with creditors. You cannot assign this problem to an accountant or a clerk in your office. This is something that only you can do, and it is a key responsibility of your leadership position.

To accelerate cash influx into your business, go to your customers who owe you money and ask them to pay you immediately.

If necessary, give them discounts and bonuses for immediate payment. Often, you can get them to buy your products and services in advance of their requirements by giving them a special price if they pay you immediately. Many people have pulled themselves out of a financial crunch by simply contacting their best customers personally and asking for their help.

Get Tough If You Must

If your financial problems have been caused or exacerbated by customers who have not paid, go and visit them personally and ask for payment. Remember, this is a *crunch point*. Be prepared to threaten them with court action if they do not pay. Under our commercial laws, the failure to pay a bill when it is due entitles the creditor to go to court and petition the debtor company into bankruptcy. The courts tend to move quickly to shut down a company that is not paying its bills.

Usually, a company will find the money to get rid of you if the alternative is to have its doors closed by the sheriff.

Above all, you must be courageous and aggressive in communicating and contacting the key people who are or can be affected by your financial problems. Don't be ashamed or embarrassed, no more than a soldier who's been wounded on the battlefield would be ashamed or embarrassed about a wound. It is a normal, natural, and unavoidable experience that goes along with the job.

Crunch Point Actions

1. Identify the key people outside of your business whose continuing support and patronage you need to survive and prosper. Be sure that you keep them informed if their financial stake in your company is in danger.

2. Identify the key people inside your business and tell them clearly what is going on and what you are doing to deal with it. Practice a "No Surprises" policy with everyone.

"A man can rise above his circumstances and achieve whatever he sets his mind to, if he exercises unshakable persistence and a positive mental attitude."

—SAMUEL SMILES

Identify Your Constraints

"Obstacles will look large or small to you according to whether you are large or small."

—ORISON SWETT MARDEN

Between wherever you are today and wherever you want to be in the future, there is something—often several things—that are holding you back. For you to get out of the crunch you are in and achieve your business and personal goals, you must identify your *constraints*, those factors that are restricting your progress.

The starting point of constraint analysis is for you to be absolutely clear about your goals. What is it that you want to achieve, avoid, or preserve? If it is financial, what specific amount of money do you need to generate, and in what time period? The greater clarity you have about exactly what it is you want, the easier it will be for you to determine the best way to achieve it.

Write your goal down, using the present tense. For example, you could write, "My goal is to generate $50,000 in cash by May 31." This type of goal is measurable and specific. This level of clarity makes it easy for you to determine how close you are to achieving the goal. And it includes a deadline that you can measure your progress against.

Once you have determined your goal, make a list of the steps that you will have to take to achieve that goal. What are the various things that you must do to get from where you are to where you want to go?

Identify the Main Constraint

Once you have a goal and a plan, you then ask yourself, "What is the limiting factor in achieving this goal?" What is your main constraint or bottleneck? Another way to phrase this question is, *"Why aren't I already at my goal?"*

Your goal may be a certain level of productivity, a certain level of sales, or a certain level of gross or net profit. The main constraint may be mechanical, manpower, financial, sales, or customers. There is always one main constraint or choke point that determines the *speed* at which you achieve your most important goal. Your job is to identify that constraint clearly so that you can go to work to alleviate it.

Do an Internal Analysis First

When it comes to constraint analysis, you will find that 80 percent of your constraints will be internal; they will be inside of yourself or your company. Only 20 percent of your constraints will be external, outside yourself and your business.

Start the process of constraint analysis by asking, "What is it in me or my business that is holding me back from achieving my goal?" In many cases, you will find that the main constraint between you and your goal is a fear of failure or a fear of rejection. This fear is holding you back from taking the actions necessary to accomplish what you want and need.

Your deep-rooted fears and doubts are often manifested or expressed in your excuses. Very often, your excuses are cleverly formulated reasons that you inadvertently use to position yourself as a victim, a person who has no choice or control over what is going on. When you make excuses or blame others, you let yourself off the hook. You absolve yourself from ever having to do anything to correct your situation. Don't let this happen to you.

Test Your Excuses

There is a way that you can test your excuses to see if they are valid. It is simply to ask yourself, "Is there anyone else who has my same excuse but who is moving ahead and succeeding nonetheless?"

If you are honest with yourself, you will immediately realize that there are hundreds of thousands, if not millions, of people who have it worse than you could ever imagine but are succeeding anyway. If this is the case, your excuse is invalid. Don't let it hold you back anymore.

Identify External Constraints

The second type of constraint, which accounts for the other 20 percent of bottlenecks, is external. Such constraints are contained in the actions or nonactions of other people. These external constraints may have to do with markets, customers, sales, bank approvals, payments of receivables, and other factors. Even if your main constraints are external and therefore somewhat outside of your control, there is almost always something that you can do to address them and deal with them in some way.

As an exercise, engage in what I call "no-limit thinking." Imagine for a moment that you have no limitations of knowledge or skill, friends or contacts, money or resources. Imagine that you can do, be, and have anything you want in life. If this were the case, what actions would you take immediately?

What one great goal would you set for yourself if you knew you could not fail? If you were absolutely guaranteed of success in any goal, small or large, short term or long term, what one goal would you set for yourself? What would be the first step that you would take toward the accomplishment of this goal?

Focus on Your Main Constraint

Once you have identified your main constraint in each area of activity, focus single-mindedly, like a laser beam, on alleviating that one constraint. Don't busy yourself with little problems around the edges. Focus on the one major limit that is holding you back more than any other factor. Removing this constraint can assist you in the achievement of your most important goal faster than anything else you can do. Get on with it.

Crunch Point Actions

1.   Determine the most important goal that you could accomplish right now, the one goal that could have the greatest positive impact on your current situation.

2.   Determine the critical constraint or bottleneck that determines the *speed* at which you attain that goal. What could you do to alleviate it?

"Always bear in mind that your own resolution to succeed is more important than any other one thing."

—ABRAHAM LINCOLN

Unleash Your Creativity

"Do not pray for tasks equal to your powers.
Pray for powers equal to your tasks."

—PHILLIPS BROOKS

You have within you *right now* all the mental resources and abilities you need to solve any problem or resolve any crisis you will ever have to deal with. Your job is to unleash these mental powers and focus them single-mindedly on getting through a crunch point as quickly as possible.

Sometimes I ask my audiences, "What is the highest paid work in America?" They respond with all kinds of answers, from politician to public speaker to trial lawyer. Then I give the real answer.

The highest paid work in America is *thinking*. Your ability to think clearly and well, and to use your mind to solve problems and make decisions, can add more value to your life, and to the lives of others, than any other activity you can engage in. Thomas Edison described this form of concentrated brainpower as "the ability to apply your physical and mental energies to one problem incessantly without growing weary."

Consider the Consequences

Here is an important point. You can tell how valuable an action is by measuring the potential consequences of doing it or not doing it. Analyzing the potential consequences of any action or behavior is a good way of setting priorities. Something that is important has large potential consequences. Something that is of low or no value has no real consequences. It doesn't matter whether you do it or not.

Thinking accurately can have the greatest potential consequences of anything you do on an hour-by-hour, day-by-day basis. One good thought, idea, or insight can change your life, especially in the middle of crunch time. That's why unleashing your creativity is the key to accomplishing extraordinary things for yourself and your family.

Albert Einstein wrote that "every child is born a genius." In reality, you are born a *potential* genius. You have within you the ability to solve any problem and achieve any goal, but you must *use* your creativity for it to do you any good.

Your Creativity Increases with Practice

Creativity is like a muscle. It grows stronger with use. The more ideas you generate to solve your problems and improve your life, the more ideas you will come up with later. By harnessing your creative powers, you actually become smarter in terms of your ability to improve your life and work in multiple ways.

The true definition of creativity is simply "improvement." Any time you use your mind to change the way something is done to improve its performance in some way, you are engaging in pure creativity. When you face a crunch point in your life or work, it is more important than ever before that you tap into your creative powers to solve your problems and make better decisions.

Organize Your Thinking

Here is a simple way to unlock your creativity. It requires that you use your mind in an organized fashion.

Begin by asking, "What, exactly, is the problem?" If you are working by yourself, write down a clear statement of the problem on a piece of paper. If you are working with a group, write a clear statement of the problem on a whiteboard where everyone can read it.

Once everyone is in agreement on the definition of the problem, you then ask the magic question: "What *else* is the problem?"

Beware of any problem for which there is only *one* definition.

For example, often the definition of the problem is something like this: "Our sales are too low." When you ask, "What else is the problem?" the answer may be that "the sales of our competitors are too high." When you ask what else could be the problem, the answer might be that "customers prefer the products of our competitors to ours."

Ask the question again and you'll get the answer, "We are not selling enough of our products in comparison with our competitors."

In my consulting and coaching work, I have developed twenty-one "what else" questions for sales analysis. Whichever definition of the problem the group I'm working with settles on determines the type of solution that we will implement, from improving the product to increasing the advertising to upgrading the skills of the sales force. But we must be clear about the problem before we embark on any solution.

Identify the Correct Solution

Once you have agreed on the *real* problem, which is very seldom the *obvious* problem, the next question you ask is, "What is the ideal solution to this problem?"

The first solution may again be obvious: "Increase sales!" But you discipline yourself to then ask the "what else" question once more. What else is the solution to this problem? Again, the rule is to beware of any problem for which there is only *one* solution.

The more ways you define the problem, the more you'll be able to define the solution in ways that are better and more creative. You can increase the likelihood of solving the problem by ten times, twenty times, or even fifty times by simply stating the problem and the solution correctly.

Practice "Mindstorming" on Your Problem

Another powerful way to unlock your creativity is the twenty-idea method, or what's called *mindstorming*. This is the most powerful single method of creative thinking and problem solving ever discovered. I receive letters and e-mails every week from people who have used it to transform their business and personal lives.

Here's how it works. Take your main goal or problem and write it in the form of a question. For example, if your goal is to generate an extra $50,000 by the end of the month, you can write it as a question: "What can we do to generate an extra $50,000 within the next thirty days?"

You then discipline yourself to write out a minimum of twenty answers to your question. You can write out more than twenty answers, but this seems to be the magic number for triggering maximum creativity.

The first three to five answers will be easy. The next five to ten answers will be hard, and the last series of answers will be incredibly difficult. But time after time, people tell me that it is the twentieth answer that is the breakthrough solution that they have been seeking, sometimes for many months.

Take Action Immediately

Once you have generated twenty answers to your question, select at least *one answer* and take action on it immediately, as quickly as possible. There is something about taking immediate action that keeps the river of creativity flowing through your mind. For the next few hours, your mind will sparkle like Christmas tree lights, throwing out insights and ideas that often lead to major breakthroughs.

Be prepared to accept feedback and self-correct. No matter how good the idea sounds, it may be just the first move in a longer game. Sometimes, by trying a new idea, you get immediate feedback that enables you to correct the idea and try something else. Often the solution turns out to be several degrees removed from the initial idea, but it was your taking action on the first idea that caused the domino effect that led to the solution you were seeking.

Never forget; you are a *potential genius*. And the way that you unleash your creativity is by focusing your mental energies on one single problem at a time using one of these methods. Try them and see.

Crunch Point Actions

1. Take your biggest problem today and write it in the form of a question requiring a solution. For example: How can we increase our profits by 50 percent over the next twelve months?

2. Once you have defined your biggest problem, ask, "What else is the problem?" and "What else is the solution?"

"The rewards for those who persevere far exceed the pain that must precede the victory."

—TED W. ENGSTROM

CHAPTER 11

Focus on Key Result Areas

"It is not the situation that makes the man,
but the man who makes the situation."

—FREDERICK W. ROBERTSON

One of the major reasons that you get into a crunch in the first place is that you get away from the basic activities that made you successful in the beginning.

Sometimes, the most helpful thing you can do is to remember the little things that you have forgotten in the growth and development of your business. For example, every business begins with certain core competencies possessed by the business owners and key employees. What are yours?

Your core competencies are the things that you do especially well, better than 90 percent of your competitors. Your original product or service is an extension of your core competencies into the marketplace. You use them to produce a product or service that you can sell and deliver at a price that people are willing to pay.

In dealing with the inevitable problems, disappointments, and reversals of business life, you must continually ask, What are we good at? What do we do better than anyone else? What has been the major reason for our success to date?

Your Success Comes from a Few Things

Remember, 80 percent of your results comes from 20 percent of what you do. In other words, 80 percent of your profits comes from 20 percent of your products and services; 80 percent of your productivity comes from 20 percent of your people; 80 percent of your success comes from 20 percent of your activities, and so on. You must stand back and be clear about the top 20 percent in each area when you face a sudden reversal in your business.

Start with your area of *specialization*. In what customers, markets, or products do you specialize and focus your time, attention, and efforts? If you were to ask your customers about your business and your area of focus, what would they say? A major reason for business problems is the tendency to expand out of your areas of specialization into areas where you are not as good.

How Are You Different and Better?

What is your area of *differentiation*? This is the key to success in business. What is it that you offer to your customers that none of your competitors can offer? What is it that your business does for your customers that makes you special in some way? The rule is: If you don't have competitive advantage, don't compete.

One of your greatest responsibilities is to either determine or develop your area of differentiation, your competitive advantage, and then focus all of your marketing and sales efforts in that area. What is it that you, and only you, can do for your customers that no other company can offer? What is your "unique selling proposition?"

Each company has to have an area of excellence. What is yours? This is something in which you excel and that is important and valuable to your customers.

Every individual must have one or more areas of excellence as well. What is it that you do, or could do, better than anyone else in your business? The development and exploitation of your competitive advantage and your area of excellence is the key to getting through crunch time. Sometimes, just reverting to what it is that you do extremely well for your customers can turn your situation around.

Protecting Your Core

Practice the "citadel strategy" in your business. Imagine that your business is like a besieged city. You have to withdraw step-by-step from the outer walls to the inner walls and finally to the citadel, the most important and protected part of your city. Here are the eight key points to finding and protecting your core:

1. Your citadel consists of your most important *products and services* that are most responsible for your growth and profitability today. If you had to drop most of your products and services, what would be the one or two that you would hold onto if you wanted to survive and eventually succeed in the current market?

2. Identify your *key people*. Who are the 20 percent of your staff that produce most of your results? Who are the bankers, suppliers, vendors, and customers who are most responsible for the success of your business? What should you do immediately to ensure that they remain loyal and supportive of you?

3. What are your *core marketing activities*? What are the things that you do that bring in the greatest number of

qualified prospects? What do you need to do to focus more of your time and resources in these areas?

4. What are your most important *selling avenues*? These are the processes, people, and methods that generate the highest and most predictable levels of sales, revenue, and cash flow. What are they, and what do you need to do to maximize your results from them?

5. What are your *key profit centers*? What are the 20 percent of your business activities that generate 80 percent of your profits? What should you do immediately to reinforce these areas?

6. Who are your *top customers*? These are the most important customers you have, the ones who buy the most, pay the most predictably, and represent the greatest source of your profits. What do you need to do to ensure that they are on board with you during your period of crisis?

7. Think of your own *personal skills, qualities, and attributes*. What one thing could you do all day long that would contribute the most to the success and survival of your business? How could you reorganize your time so that you are spending more time every day doing the few things that make the greatest contribution to your business?

8. Finally, it is essential that you identify the *key result areas* of your business, and the particular results that you must achieve every day, week, and month in order to make sales, deliver products, and collect revenues. Where are you strong? Where are you weak? What do you need to do immediately to strengthen and reinforce your weakest key result area?

If you expect to get through crunch time, your ability to select your key result areas and focus your energy and resources on your areas of competitive advantage is essential.

Crunch Point Actions

1. Determine your most important and profitable products, services, and activities and focus your time and energy on them.

2. Determine your most important customers, markets, and selling methods and dedicate 80 percent of your time and money to maximizing your results with them.

> "The most essential factor is persistence, the determination never to allow your energy or enthusiasm to be dampened by the discouragement that must inevitably come."
>
> **—JAMES WHITCOMB RILEY**

CHAPTER 12

Concentrate on Priorities

"Little minds are subdued by misfortunes;
but great minds rise above them."

—WASHINGTON IRVING

When you hit a crunch point, your ability to focus and concentrate can make all the difference between success and failure. You cannot do everything, but you can do one or two things—the most important things—and you can stay with them until they are satisfactorily completed. This is essential to getting through the crunch.

Johann Wolfgang von Goethe said, "The things that matter most must never be at the mercy of the things that matter least."

Stephen Covey said, "The main thing is to make the main thing the main thing."

There is a rule that says that every minute spent in planning saves ten minutes in execution. The time you take at the beginning to think about what you are going to do, *before* you start, ensures that when you do begin work, you will be focusing on that activity that can have the greatest possible consequences for yourself and your business.

Refuse to "major in minors." Keep asking yourself, "What's really important here?" Your ability to ask and answer this question will keep you on track and often get you out of the crunch.

Think on Paper

To keep yourself focused on your top priorities, there is a series of steps you can take. First of all, think on paper. Writing things down is absolutely essential for you to be able to take control of the situation during the emergency or crisis. Before you take any action, make a list of everything that you have to do to solve the problem and get through the crunch.

In 1342 A.D., the philosopher William of Occam developed a concept that has come to be known as Occam's Razor. This principle says that, in dealing with any problem or complex issue, the simplest and most direct explanation or solution is usually the correct one.

What this means is that you should refuse to allow yourself to become overwhelmed with trivia and detail. Instead, start off by trying the simplest possible solution. For example, the deadline for a major payment is looming and you don't have the money. Often, the simplest and most direct way to solve this financial problem is to go straight to the creditor and ask for additional time. If you are short of cash, sometimes the simplest and most direct way is to go to your biggest customer and ask him to pay you in advance for products or services that he is going to buy in the future.

Sometimes, the simplest solution to a business problem is to fire a person, or step in and take complete charge of the situation yourself. Often it is to decide to walk away from a situation that cannot be saved. Always look for the most direct and simple way to get through the crunch.

Make a List

At the beginning of your day, make a list of everything that you have to do during that day. Go over the list and number the top seven items. Ask yourself, "If I could do only one thing on this list today, which one task would it be?" Put a "1" next to that task or activity. Repeat this exercise until you have your major tasks organized from one to seven.

Then, discipline yourself to start immediately on your number-one task and to work at it with single-minded concentration until it is complete. Refuse to do anything else but that one thing. If you are called away or distracted, immediately return to that task, like a gyroscope returns to center, and begin working on it again. Invariably, this one task can have the greatest potential consequences in your job or situation.

Practice Triage on Your Work

In concentrating on priorities during a crunch point, use the triage method. This method was developed by the French army in World War I, when the dressing stations behind the lines were swamped with far too many wounded soldiers for the doctors and nurses to treat. They solved the problem by dividing the wounded into three groups. The first were those who would die, no matter how much treatment they received. They were put aside and made comfortable.

The second group included those who had only light wounds. They would survive whether they got immediate treatment or not. They also were put aside. The third group consisted of those soldiers who would survive *only* if they were treated immediately. This is where the doctors and nurses focused their attention.

In your business you should apply triage as well. Focus all your attention on those problems that can be solved if you act immediately. Refuse to worry about situations that cannot be resolved. Let them go. And don't waste time on situations that will take care of themselves whether you do anything or not. Focus on those problems, decisions, and activities where immediate action is essential to saving the situation.

What's Important Here?

During crunch time, keep asking yourself key questions: What is really important in this situation? Of all the things I could do, if I could do only one thing, what would it be? What does this situation need of me that only I can contribute?

Here are the two best questions to keep you on track. The first is, "What can I, and only I, do that if done well, will make a real difference?" The second question, which you must ask and answer over and over again, is: "What is the most valuable use of my time right now?"

Whatever your answers to these questions, discipline yourself to work on that priority, and only that, until it is complete. By focusing and concentrating on your highest priorities, you will be more productive and effective in helping yourself and your company out of the crisis.

Crunch Point Actions

1.   Identify the one thing that only you can do, which if done well, will make a real difference in getting you through your current problem.

2.   Cut to the chase! What is the simple, obvious step you can take immediately to eliminate the crunch?

"Do what you can, with what you have, right where you are."
—THEODORE ROOSEVELT

C H A P T E R 1 3

Counterattack!

"We are no longer puppets being manipulated by outside powerful forces; we become the powerful force ourselves."

—LEO BUSCAGLIA

When the you-know-what hits the fan and the survival of your business is endangered, you must begin thinking like a military commander in battle. Often the situation is so serious that you have to step forward and make hard decisions, and make them immediately. No more Mr. Nice Guy.

Top military leaders have been studied going back to 600 B.C. Over the centuries, several principles of military strategy that lead to victory or defeat have been identified. They are now taught to student officers in every military school in the world. By applying these principles of military strategy to your life and your business, you can often turn the situation around and achieve extraordinary results.

Strategy 1: Be Clear in Your Objective

The first principle of military strategy is the Principle of the Objective. It requires that you be perfectly clear about the goal (or goals) that you want and need to get through a crunch point. In business, the practice of this principle usually is focused on goals related to sales, revenues, and cash flow. You need plans, schedules, and the right people doing the right jobs to achieve your most important objectives. Everyone should be absolutely clear about what they are expected to do, and they must be committed to success, to victory, no matter how serious the crisis.

Strategy 2: Take Bold Action

The second strategic principle is the Principle of the Offensive. It requires that you take action—that you move forward boldly to confront your difficulties and solve your problems. As Napoleon said, "No great battles are ever won on the defensive."

Since your natural tendency when you hit crunch time is to withdraw, cut back, and play it safe, you must resist this urge and instead dare to go forward, to seize control of the situation, and to attack your difficulties with firmness and decisiveness.

Whenever one of my companies has experienced a cash crunch, my mantra is, *"When in doubt, sell your way out."* You cannot cost-cut your way out of a financial crisis. You have to generate revenues, and the only way to do that is by selling something to someone. Always think in terms of generating revenues from sales. Become very aggressive and focused in this area. Every single company that rebounded from a crisis, including companies like IBM in 1991, turned itself around by focusing single-mindedly on generating sales revenues. You should do the same.

Strategy 3: Concentrate Your Resources

The third strategic principle is the Principle of the Mass. It requires that you concentrate your best people, your best energies, and your limited resources in those areas where the greatest victories are possible. Restructure and reorganize your activities so that your best talents are focused on those results that can get you out of the crunch faster than any others.

Strategy 4: Stay Flexible

The fourth strategic principle is the Principle of the Maneuver. Almost all great battlefield successes are the result of the winning general outmaneuvering his enemy by attacking from the flank or the rear. In business, the practice of this principle requires that you try something new, and if that doesn't work, try something else. Be flexible and creative in your approach. Think of doing exactly the opposite of what you have done up until now. Keep all your options open. Survival and victory are your only considerations.

Strategy 5: Gather All Available Information

The fifth principle of military strategy is the Principle of Intelligence. We talked about this earlier, in Chapter 4. Intelligence means that you must get the facts about the situation. Learn everything you can. Ask questions, phone people, go onto the Internet. The more and better information you have, the better and more effective decisions you will be able to make.

Strategy 6: Get Everyone Working Together

The sixth principle for victory is Concerted Action. Make sure everyone on your team is working together with common goals, common values, and clearly understood work assignments. Everyone should know what is going on and what everyone else is doing. One of the rules for military victory is that you never trust to luck or wish that something will turn up. Hope is not a strategy. Look to yourself and don't expect an easy victory.

Napoleon was once asked if he believed in luck in warfare. He replied, "Yes, I believe in luck. I believe in bad luck, and I believe that I will always have it. I therefore plan accordingly."

You should do the same. If you do have a streak of good luck, consider yourself blessed. But don't count on it or hope for it to happen.

Strategy 7: You're the Boss!

The seventh principle of military strategy is Unity of Command. Everyone must know that you are completely in command. You are in charge. You are calling the shots. Everyone reports to you and answers to you. You can go back to democratic consensus later, but during crunch time, it must be clear to everyone that you are the boss.

Finally, in taking action to resolve a crisis, perhaps the most important quality you can have is a *total commitment* to success, to winning, to overcoming your difficulties, no matter what they are. The key to victory is for you to go on the attack, relentlessly moving forward. It has been said that boldness and audacity will get you into a lot of problems, but more boldness and audacity will get you out of your problems as well. Take action immediately, and keep on taking action until you win.

Crunch Point Actions

1.   Identify the goal you must attain, usually financial, to resolve the crisis and get out of the crunch. Be sure that everyone is clear on this one objective.

2.   Discipline yourself to focus single-mindedly on this number-one target, resisting the temptations to clear up small things first.

"Success seems to be largely a matter of hanging on after others have let go."

—WILLIAM FEATHER

C H A P T E R   1 4

Generate Cash Flow

*"Man is not the creature of circumstances; circumstances
are the creatures of man. We are free agents, and man is
more powerful than matter."*

—BENJAMIN DISRAELI

The single most important consideration in any business is cash flow. It is like blood or oxygen to the brain. It is the vital difference between life and death, success or failure of the enterprise.

A crunch point is most often triggered by an unexpected interruption in cash flow that threatens the very survival of the business. Your ability to deal with an interruption in cash flow is the mark of your intelligence and ability as a businessperson or business owner. This is the real test that decides whether you are truly capable of business success.

Cash flow problems can be caused by several different factors. Whatever the cause, you must immediately go into emergency mode and practice everything that we talked about in the earlier chapters. Stay calm. Get the facts. Take control. Cut your losses. Communicate constantly with the key people inside and outside of your business.

When Revenues Drop Unexpectedly

The major reason for a drop in cash flow is usually traceable to the sales department. The sales that you needed for survival and growth failed to materialize for some reason. Often the fastest way to get out of a cash crunch is to get out on the street and begin selling more of your product and getting paid for it right away.

A cash crunch can be caused by the failure of a customer to pay or a breakdown in your process of collecting receivables from people who owe you money. As a result, you are not short of assets; you are merely short of cash. This situation can be fatal, nonetheless.

Sometimes an expected bank loan or investment of some kind fails to come through, or does not come through on the schedule that you had hoped for. You go through all your cash in anticipation of the incoming funds that fail to arrive.

Carefully Analyze Your Situation

When you have a cash crunch, the first thing you should do is to sit down and do a careful analysis of your situation. Find out *exactly* how much cash you have at the present moment, in all forms, from all sources.

Find out how much you have coming in over the next thirty days, but leave nothing to chance. Never make assumptions. If an amount of incoming money is critical to your survival, get on top of it and stay on top of it. Remember, hope is not a strategy, and you must never trust to luck.

Find out how much cash is going out today, and for the next few days and weeks. Like the process of triage, stop the bleeding whenever possible. Stop making payments that consume cash. Creditors and suppliers may be temporarily unhappy, but they are dealing with an inconvenience while you are dealing with survival.

Stop all payments except those that are critical to keeping your doors open, such as rent, utilities, payroll, and taxes. Everything else can be delayed or deferred.

Ask for Breathing Room

When I started a business several years ago, I was overly optimistic about sales and not properly attentive to expenses. As a result, I quickly burned through all my savings, and everything I could borrow from my friends. I ran out of cash. The phone rang constantly with people demanding payment. My landlord threatened to seize my car. It was a nightmare.

I decided to treat my business like a turnaround, as if it was on the verge of going broke and I was threatened with losing everything. I called up or visited each of my creditors and explained my situation. I asked them to back off and give me some breathing room. To my amazement, every single one of them was sympathetic and agreed to be patient. With the breathing room they gave me, I was able to generate sales and cash flow and turn my business around.

Confront the Situation

If your situation is desperate enough in terms of running out of cash, you can use desperate measures. One time, when I ran out of cash (which happens on a regular basis when you are building a business), I called my major creditors and told them that I had two choices. I could declare bankruptcy or I could work out a long-term payment plan with them. If they pressured me and I declared bankruptcy, they would not receive a penny of the amounts that I owed them. But if they worked with me for the next few months, I promised to repay everything. Without exception, faced with that kind of threat, they all agreed to back off and give me enough time to turn my business around—which I did.

Growing businesses consume enormous amounts of cash, far more than you expect. You will be hit continually with unexpected expenses and losses, such as customers who don't pay you. Everything costs more than you budgeted for and takes longer to process than you expected. It is only after a business has been in operation for a few years that fluctuations in cash flow smooth out and are easier to manage. Just remember, "When the going gets tough, the tough get going."

Look for Cash Everywhere

When you run into a cash crunch, gauge everything that you can possibly do to generate cash in the short term to ensure survival. Many entrepreneurs, including myself, have withdrawn every penny possible that was available on their credit cards. Once I even took out a loan on my car, a Mercedes that I owned free and clear, and got enough money to get me through that month.

Be creative. Turn everything you can into cash, at least temporarily. Forget your pride; be willing to beg and borrow from anyone who has money. Just as a military commander is absolutely committed to victory, as a business owner, you must be absolutely committed to *survival*.

Saving Federal Express

Many years ago, when Fred Smith was building Federal Express, the company ran out of cash. He had struggled for years and had finally hit the wall. He could not even make payroll. The people around him told him that he had fought the good fight and it was now time to give up. Every single source of borrowing had been exhausted, and there was nothing that could be done.

In one of the most incredible acts of entrepreneurial courage in American business history, Smith took the last bit of cash that the company had and booked the night plane for Las Vegas. He walked into a Las Vega casino, sat down at the gaming tables, and played for twenty-four hours straight, winning enough money to make payroll and keep the company alive for another month. He then took his winnings and caught the next plane back.

Smith's story is a reminder that you should not overlook any move—no matter how daring, off the wall, or even desperate it may seem—in taking action to solve your cash flow problems.

Crunch Point Actions

1. If you are facing a cash crunch, immediately sit down and analyze your finances, determining how much you have, how much you owe, and what monies you can tap into from any source.

2. Conserve cash at all costs. Delay, defer, and put off payments. At the same time, ask for advance payment from everyone, both current and future customers.

"Never give up; never, never, never give up."
—WINSTON CHURCHILL

CHAPTER 15

Care for Your Customers

*"Nothing splendid has ever been achieved except by
those who dared believe that something inside of them
was superior to circumstance."*

—BRUCE BARTON

The purpose of a business is to create and keep customers. Many people think that the purpose of a business is to make profits, but profits are merely the result of creating customers in a cost-effective way. All effective businesses and all top business owners focus their time, attention, and energy constantly on customer creation.

The single most important measure of business success is your level of *customer satisfaction*. The more and better you satisfy your customers with what they want and need at prices they are willing to pay, the more they will buy from you and recommend you to their friends. Customer satisfaction must therefore be the focal point of all your business activities.

Sales, revenues, cash flow, and business success are the direct result of satisfying customers in sufficient quantity at a profit to you. When you hit a crunch point, satisfied customers can be the key to your survival.

The Customer Is Always Right

There are two rules for business success with regard to customers. Rule number one is, "The customer is always right." Rule number two is, "When in doubt, refer back to rule number one."

When we say that the "customer is always right," it means that what the customer wants, needs, demands, and is willing to pay for determines business activity. Customers are selfish, demanding, vain, fickle, and disloyal, just like you when you are a customer. But they are always right. You may think they are wrong in a given situation, but if you lose their business, then it is you who is wrong.

For this reason, customers are like a moving target, so you must continually adjust and modify your offerings and activities to satisfy your customers, or they will go somewhere else.

Customers Can Choose

Customers always have three choices in the market:

- They can buy from you.
- They can buy from someone else.
- They can refrain from buying at all.

Your primary goal in sales is to get people to buy from you rather than from your competitors. Then, you must take such good care of them that they buy from you again and, finally, recommend you to their friends.

Most business success comes from developing such a good

reputation in the marketplace that your customers tell others how happy they are that they bought from you. This is called *word-of-mouth advertising,* and it is the most powerful form of advertising that exists today.

When you treat your customers so well that they become your advocates, your success is assured. They will then enthusiastically encourage the people they know to buy from you as well. You can always tell how well you are doing in business by measuring the number of customers who buy from you repeatedly and the amount of business that you get from referrals and testimonials.

Get Back to Basics

If your sales slow down, you must step back and analyze your business in four key results areas (as mentioned previously in Chapter 11): specialization, differentiation, segmentation, and customer focus.

First, be absolutely clear about your area of *specialization.* The natural tendency of most companies is to diffuse their efforts and spread their energies over a wide area rather than focusing on specialized areas where they can be successful. The three primary areas of specialization available to you are type of customer, type of product or service, or geographical area. What is your area of specialization?

The second key to sales analysis is to determine your area of *differentiation.* This is the feature or benefit of your product or service that makes it superior and more desirable to that of anything else offered by your competitors. You must be absolutely clear about what it is that you do for your customer that no one else does, and then build all your marketing, advertising, and sales activities around that.

Focus on Your Best Prospects

The third key to increasing your sales is *segmentation.* This requires that you define your ideal customer profile, your target market. You must be absolutely clear about the particular customer type who most values what you do so well in your area of specialization. This is the customer who will buy the soonest and pay the most for what you sell.

Finally, once you are clear about your areas of specialization, differentiation, and segmentation, you must then *focus and concentrate* on just those customers who are most likely to buy from you the soonest. All of your sales and marketing problems will be a result of your deviating from these four basic principles.

Do More Face-to-Face Selling

Most business crunches can be traced back to low sales, to a drop-off of sales revenues and cash flow. The solution to most business problems is high sales, or a rapid increase in sales and cash flow. When in doubt, sell yourself out.

Albert Einstein once said that "nothing happens until something moves." In business you could say, "Nothing happens until someone sells something to somebody."

Apply the 80/20 rule to your selling activities. Spend 80 percent of your time engaging face-to-face with new prospective customers and only 20 percent of the time doing everything else. Unless you have a retail store that is open for specific hours, you will find that most salespeople are performing nonsales activities a majority of the time. You can increase your sales, revenues, and profitability by doubling and tripling the amount of time that you are out there making direct contact with people who can buy from you.

Answer Customer Questions

Customers always want to know the answers to two basic questions with regard to your product or service. First, "Why should I buy this product or service at all?" and, second, "Why should I buy it from you?" You must be able to answer these questions in twenty-five words or less in the first thirty seconds of your sales conversation or meeting with the customer.

Customers also want to know the answers to four more questions with regard to your product or service: What does it cost? What do I get? How fast do I get it? How sure can I be that I will get what you say I will get for the amount of money you are going to charge me? If you fail to answer any one of these questions satisfactorily, the sale will not take place.

Ask the Fundamental Sales Question

There is one big sales question that you can use in your business and with your products and services for the rest of your career. It is:

> What exactly is to be sold, and to whom is it to be sold, and by whom, and how is it to be sold, priced, and paid for, and how is it to be produced, delivered, and serviced?

Your ability to ask and answer each of the multiple questions within this fundamental question, and then to weave your answers into a complete sales presentation and business process, is your key to sales success. It is amazing how many business owners have never really considered this question and are unclear about the correct answers.

It is worth repeating: Business success comes from *high sales*. The fastest way to get through a business crunch is to focus single-mindedly on generating more and better sales to more and better customers.

Crunch Point Actions

1. Identify your top-selling and most profitable products and services; then concentrate your best people on selling more of them to your best prospective customers.

2.   Review your sales process and methodology and look for ways to make it more persuasive and convincing.

"Few things are impossible to diligence and skill. Great works are performed not by strength, but by perseverance."
—SAMUEL JOHNSON

Close More Sales

*"This is where you will win the battle,
in the playhouse of your mind."*

—MAXWELL MALTZ

It is amazing how many businesses go under even though they have a pipeline full of prospects who are at various stages of buying, but who have not yet made the final commitment. The key to business health is your ability to close sales, to get your prospects to make a decision, to take action on your offering, to sign the order, and to pay you.

When you find yourself in crunch time, when your financial water level drops dangerously low and you are threatened with bankruptcy, your only long-term solution is to increase your sales and revenues as fast as you can. When IBM got into trouble in the early 1990s, it took several thousand of its engineers, gave them crash courses in selling, and put them on the street with briefcases to call on customers. Within a year, the company turned around.

There's No Other Way

When your available finances drop dramatically, you cannot cost-cut your way back to solvency. No business ever became successful by reducing costs alone. It has to be in conjunction with calling on more customers and closing more sales.

Each business begins with an idea for a product or service that people want, need, and are willing to pay for. If the new business is to get off the drawing board, there must be someone in the business who is experienced and competent at selling. This is usually the entrepreneur, but sometimes it can be the first employee. Hewlett-Packard Company was started by two good friends, William Hewlett and David Packard, Hewlett being the engineering brain and Packard being the marketing and sales expert. While Hewlett developed various engineering devices, Packard went out and sold them. It became one of the best partnerships in business history. The key was selling.

An Art and a Science

Selling is both an art and a science. There is a method and process. There are seven steps in selling, like dialing seven digits to get through on a telephone. The seven parts of the sales process are:

1. Prospecting
2. Establishing rapport and trust
3. Identifying customer needs
4. Presenting your product or service
5. Answering objections
6. Closing the sale
7. Getting resales and referrals

You must perform each of these steps in order, in the proper sequence, if you want to make sales consistently.

You Need a Closer

To survive and thrive, every business must have one or more people who are absolutely excellent at selling the product. They must be fully engaged every day in generating sales. You can have the finest product or service in the world, supported by the finest company and people, but if someone is not out in the market selling it aggressively, the business will go under.

During the late 1990s, the dot-com boom spawned hundreds of companies that went public at multibillion-dollar valuations. Experienced businesspeople, like Warren Buffett, stood back and refused to invest in any of them. The problem they saw, which turned out to be the case, was that no one was selling anything to anyone and getting paid for it. Hundreds of millions of dollars were going into the businesses but no sales or profits were coming out. By the time the dust had settled, 95 percent of the dot-coms had turned into "dot bombs" and the investors had lost everything they had put in. There were no sales.

Practice the 100-Call Method

If you are suffering a business crunch because of low sales, there is a fast, effective, proven way to turn your sales results around. It is this: Make a resolution to go out and talk to a hundred potential customers as fast as you possibly can. Make it a game. Set it as a goal. Don't even worry about whether one or more of them buys at this time. Instead, focus on sales activities. Start early, work harder, and stay later if you must, but set a target to get face-to-face with a hundred prospective customers in the shortest period of time possible.

If you have several salespeople, meet every morning before the selling day begins and every evening at the end of the day. Establish each person's face-to-face contact goals for the day before they start out and review everyone's progress at the end of the day when they come back. Get everyone so busy calling on prospects that no one has any time to think about or worry about anything else.

If you do this, and I have urged this method on my client companies for twenty-five years, you will see an improvement in sales results that will amaze you. Morale will go sky high. Sales will start to pour in. Your bank account will start to fill up. The whole company will start to turn around if everyone commits to making a hundred face-to-face calls as fast as they can.

Ask for the Order

Step six in the seven parts of the sales process is "closing the sale." The very best and most profitable companies have salespeople who are masters at closing the sale. The companies in trouble may have better products and more salespeople, but because of fear of failure and rejection, they hold back from asking the customer to make a buying decision. Don't let this happen to you.

There are only three ways to increase your sales. First, you can make *more* individual sales to individual customers. Second, you can make *larger* sales with higher dollar amounts to each customer. Third, you can encourage your customers to buy from you *more frequently*. All three methods require that someone closes the sale.

Go Back to the Well

Your very best source of resales and referrals are your happy customers of today. When you face a cash crunch brought about by a drop in sales, you should immediately contact all of your best customers from the past and invite them to buy from you again today. Very often, you can solve all your cash problems by getting your already-satisfied customers to buy again and recommend their friends.

When you need to increase sales quickly, always create a sense of urgency about buying. Give your customer a good reason to buy today. If necessary, cut prices, give discounts, offer bonuses, include additional services, or provide other incentives and inducements—anything else you can think of that will cause people to buy immediately.

Sell More to Each Customer

For each sale, look for ways to increase the size of the sale, or to upsell the customer who purchases one item into purchasing another item. Look for opportunities to cross-sell, getting a customer to buy something else that complements the purchase, like selling a shirt and tie to the purchaser of a suit.

Perhaps the most important thing you can do is to focus on more and better *sales training* for everyone who sells, including yourself. There is no amount of money that you could invest in sales training that will ever be equal to the lost sales revenues that you suffer every month because your people are not trained properly.

There's Always More to Learn

One of my clients bought his top salesman a set of my *Psychology of Selling* CDs for Christmas a couple of years ago. The salesman was mildly insulted. He said, "I'm the top salesman in the company and have been for several years. Why are you giving me a set of sales training CDs?"

His boss replied, "There is always room to improve. If you increased your sales as a result of an audio learning program, it would benefit us both."

Surprise! Surprise! Over the next twelve months, by listening to and following the instructions on the audio program, this salesman increased his personal income by more than $70,000. He increased sales for his company by more than $1 million. He said afterward that he was absolutely astonished at how much he still had to learn about sales.

Increase Your Sales Quickly

The fastest way to increase your sales is to upgrade the quality of your salespeople through continuous training. In my experience working with more than 1,000 companies, you will get a return of ten times, twenty times, fifty times, even a hundred times the cost of the sales training in increased revenues within twelve months. The salesman I just mentioned increased his personal income 1,000 times the $70 cost of the audio program.

The most important word in selling is *ask*. Ask continuously. Ask for appointments. Ask for decisions. Ask for the order. Ask your customers to buy again, or to buy more. Ask for referrals. Ask courteously. Ask politely. Ask respectfully. But never be afraid to ask.

It is absolutely amazing how many business problems can be solved quickly and easily by the simple act of asking your customers to buy from you, to buy again, and to bring their friends.

Crunch Point Actions

1. Analyze your business and each of your salespeople by giving yourself and them a grade of one to ten on each of the seven key steps of selling. All of you should work on your weakest skill sets.

2. Resolve today to make a hundred new calls on new prospects as fast as you can. Don't worry about whether you make a sale or not; just concentrate on numbers.

"To get profits without risk, experience without danger, and reward without work is as impossible as it is to live without being born."

—A. P. GOUTHEY

C H A P T E R 1 7

Keep Things Simple

"It is a simple task to make things complex, but a complex task to make them simple."

—MEYER'S LAW

In normal times, you are overwhelmed with too much to do and too little time. In crunch time, you are often swamped with far more tasks than you can handle. This situation makes it almost impossible for you to develop the coolness, calmness, and self-control that you need to contend with the unexpected reversal or setback.

You really must simplify your life in every way you can, from both a personal and a business standpoint. Simplifying things now will help you weather the crunch points to come.

Start off the process by determining your true values. Decide what is really important to you. It has been said that all problems in human life can be resolved with a return to *values*. What are yours? Where might you be deviating from them? It is easy to get caught up and overwhelmed by the problems facing you. To assert control, you need to stand back and ask yourself, "What are my core beliefs?"

What do you really care about? What would you do if you learned today that you had only six months to live? How important would certain parts of your current situation be if they wouldn't really matter in the fullness of time? Take the long view.

Consider the Great Question

Ask yourself the great question: "What do I really want to do with my life?"

When 2,500 senior citizens who had reached age 100 were interviewed, each of them said that they wished that they had taken more time to reflect and think about what they had really wanted out of life, rather than simply acting and reacting throughout life. It is a good idea for you to start thinking about this question much earlier.

Set *peace of mind* as your highest goal. In the long run, nothing is worth destroying your mental and physical health over. Once you have set peace of mind as your highest goal, organize your life around it. Refuse to allow yourself to be put off your game or to become anxious or upset about whatever is going on around you. You will find this to be an extremely valuable trait to have during crunch time.

Practice the Ten-Goal Method

Here's a simple exercise to simplify things and to decide what you really want. Take a sheet of paper and write down a list of ten goals that you'd like to accomplish in the next year or sometime in the foreseeable future. Once you have written down ten goals, ask yourself this question: "If I could achieve any goal on this list within twenty-four hours, which one goal would have the greatest positive impact on my life?"

Whatever your answer to that question, put a circle around

that goal and make that your *major definite purpose*. From that moment forward, organize your time and activities around it.

Set a deadline for this goal and, if necessary, set sub-deadlines. Make a list of everything you can do to achieve this goal. Organize the list by *priority* and *sequence*. Decide what is more important and what is less important in the achievement of the goal. Determine what you need to do before you do something else. With a list of activities organized by priority and sequence, you have a *plan*. Now you are back in control.

Take Continuous Action

Once you have a major goal and a written plan, the next step is for you to take action on your plan. Do something. Do anything. From now on, work on that number-one goal, your major definite purpose, every day. Never miss a day.

Think about your goal when you get up in the morning. Visualize this one goal continually, as if it were already realized. Think about it throughout the day. Think about it in the evening and as you go off to sleep. This single-minded focus on one goal will impose a sense of order and clarity that will begin moving you rapidly toward both simplification and greater accomplishment.

Imagine $20 Million

Here is another way to clear your mind and simplify your life: Imagine that you have achieved a net worth of $20 million. But just today, you learn that you have an incurable illness and you have only ten years left to live. Here is the question: If you had $20 million in the bank and only ten years to live, how would you simplify your life? What would become more important to you, and what would be less important?

Imagine that you have no limitations on what you could do, have, or be in the future. Imagine that you have all the time and money, all the knowledge and experience, all the friends and contacts. Imagine that you have no problems or difficulties at all. What would you do differently in your current situation?

There Are Four Ways to Change Your Life

In reality, there are only four ways to change your life, personally or professionally:

1. You can do *more* of certain things. What are the things that you should do more of to improve your life or your business?

2. You can do *less* of other things. What are the things you should be doing less of if you want to simplify and get control over your life or your business?

3. You can *start* doing something new. What new things do you need to undertake to solve your problems, overcome your obstacles, and achieve your goals? What steps should you take immediately to begin working on these new tasks and activities? Often, one simple step in the direction of a new goal can simplify your life considerably.

4. You can *stop* doing certain things altogether. There are many things that you are doing today that made a lot of sense when you started them in the past. But today, they are ideal candidates for "creative abandonment." Sometimes, you can save many hours out of the day or week just by discontinuing certain activities altogether.

Eliminate Nonessential Tasks

The fact is that the only way that you can get control of your time and simplify your life is to stop doing certain things. This can be especially critical during a crunch point.

Setting priorities requires setting *posteriorities* as well. Posteriorities are things that you need to stop doing in order to free up time to do more of those things that are most important to you and your future. For each "to do" list, you need a "not to do" list as well.

One of my clients found that he was spending hours every day dealing with hundreds of e-mails, so he learned how to delegate the review of e-mails to his secretary. Together they discovered that 95 percent of those e-mails did not require his personal attention. He told me, with some amazement, that he had saved twenty-three hours a week by simply organizing, delegating, and better processing his e-mail messages.

Spend Your Time Differently

The fact is that you cannot save time. You can only *spend* time differently. You can only reallocate time away from lower-value activities toward higher-value activities. Instead of trying to do more things, you should do fewer things but things of higher value.

Another way to simplify your life is to *reengineer* your activities. That means you look for ways to reduce, condense, and consolidate the steps in a particular business process. You delegate everything you can to others who can do them as well as you. You outsource all business activities that can be done by other companies. You eliminate all low-value, no-value activities that consume time but contribute very little. You look for ways to consolidate several tasks into one job and then do it all at once.

Determine Your Hourly Rate

A good way to simplify your life is to think about your hourly rate. How much do you earn, or want to earn, each hour? For example, if your annual income goal is $50,000, divide that amount by the 2,000-hour average work year of an American businessperson. That calculation gives you an hourly rate of $25. From now on, if that is your income goal, refuse to do anything that does not pay you your desired $25 hourly rate. Refuse to do anything that someone else can do at $5 or $10 per hour. Adhering to this standard can simplify your life considerably, almost overnight.

Before you begin any task, ask yourself this question: "What if this task weren't done at all?" Here is the rule: If it is *not* necessary to do it immediately, then delay, defer, and put off any tasks you possibly can into the future, so you have more time to think and act calmly in the present.

Plan in Advance

You can simplify your life by planning your time and activities well in advance. You should plan out each month in advance. Plan out each week in advance, preferably the weekend before. Plan out each day in advance the evening before.

The method of daily planning is simple. Start by making a list of everything that you have to do the next day. Go over the list and number your tasks by priority. Put a "1" by the most important task on your list. Put a "2" by the second most important task. Do this for your top seven tasks.

When you start work in the morning, start with your number-one task and discipline yourself to stay at it. Resolve to work full-blast, with 100 percent total attention, on the one task that is more important than anything else at that moment. If you get distracted, come back to that task as quickly as you can. Practice this same "single handling" technique with the other tasks on your list as you come to them. This decision to work single-mindedly on your most important tasks will not only simplify your life, it will dramatically increase your productivity, too.

Leave Things Off

When you come home at night, a great way to simplify your life is to just "leave things off." The average person comes home and immediately turns on the television. On the way home, this person listens to the radio the entire time. The mind never gets a rest.

But when you leave things off, you create a *zone of silence* that allows your mind to become calm and clear, like the silt that settles in a bucket of water left to stand for a period of time. As a result of creating these silences, you begin to think better and with greater clarity. You become more relaxed and composed. You feel more effective and efficient.

Keep First Things First

Especially, put your *relationships* first. Put spending one-on-one time with your spouse and children ahead of all other priorities. When you sit down to dinner, leave things off. Never have the television playing when you are conversing and communing with the key people in your life.

Take excellent care of your physical health. Eat the right foods and eat in moderation. Drink lots of water. Exercise thirty minutes every day. Get lots of rest, especially when you are going through crunch time.

Finally, remember this: It is when you most feel that you have no time to relax and simplify your life that it is most important that you make the time to do so. You are your most precious asset. Take good care of yourself.

In his essay "The Fox and the Hedgehog," Isaiah Berlin says that the fox is clever because he knows many things, but the hedgehog is smarter because he knows one big thing. The one big thing that you need to know and practice during a crunch point is simplification. The act of simplifying your life will give you the space you need to solve any problem that life can throw at you.

Crunch Point Actions

1. Make a list of the three to five things that are most important to you in life, and then dedicate yourself to spending more time in those areas.

2. Make a list of ten goals, select the most important one, and then work on that goal every single day until you achieve it.

> "You must be courageous, and courage is the capacity to go from failure to failure without any loss of enthusiasm."
>
> **—WINSTON CHURCHILL**

CHAPTER 18

Conserve Your Energy

"Success in its highest and noblest form calls for peace of mind and enjoyment and happiness, which come only to the man who has found the work that he likes best."

—NAPOLEON HILL

When you are experiencing a crunch point in your business or in your personal life, you must make it a priority to take excellent care of yourself physically, mentally, and emotionally. During a crisis, you will often be overloaded with stress, with too much to do and too little time to do it. You can very easily become overtired, even exhausted.

But in crunch time, you are like an athlete in an important competition. Just as athletes eat the right foods, get the right exercise, and get lots of rest, you must do the same. The more rested you are, and the better foods you eat, the greater energy and clarity you will have, the more creative you will be, and the better decisions you will make.

Your ability to think clearly and act decisively is what you need to get through the crunch point. As Vince Lombardi once said, "Fatigue makes cowards of us all."

Get Lots of Sleep

The fact is that if you are living a busy life, you need a minimum of seven to eight hours of sleep each night. Most Americans get by on six to seven hours, sometimes less. As a result, more than half the workforce in America, though seemingly awake and alert, is actually functioning in a kind of mental fog. They may be present and going through the motions, but they are not as sharp and alert as they could be.

There is nothing more important in helping you to get through a crunch point than for you to get lots of rest. Eat earlier and allow at least three hours between your dinner and bedtime. Turn off the television and aim to get to bed by 10:00 P.M. Many people have told me that the simple act of getting a full eight hours of sleep each night has transformed their lives.

By sleeping eight hours, you will have more energy, eat less, and be more alert, more positive, more cheerful, more resilient, and more capable of dealing with the challenges and difficulties you face in crunch time.

Recharge Your Batteries

Crunch points often drain you *emotionally*, leaving you worn out and not capable of functioning at your best. It's almost as though your levels of emotional energy are equivalent to the energy levels of a battery. The more emotional adversity you have, the more you drain your emotional batteries until, finally, you lose your ability to make good decisions. Don't let this happen to you.

Sometimes, the very best thing you can do during crunch

time, especially when you feel that you have no time at all, is to back off completely. Take a full day off where you do nothing whatever that is associated with business. Sleep in late and get fully rested. Go for a walk or to a movie. Go out for dinner. Completely relax.

Shut Down Completely

Here's what I've learned from experience. For you to recharge your mental, emotional, and physical batteries, you must shut down completely. You cannot make phone calls, study material from the office, work on your computer, or hold business meetings. You must use your strength of character and discipline to hold yourself back from doing anything at all.

This is extraordinarily difficult to do the first few times, especially if you are the workaholic type, but if you give yourself the equivalent of a Sabbath, where you shut down completely from 6:00 P.M. on Friday until Sunday morning, you will arise and emerge with double or triple the amount of energy you had before. You will be able to accomplish extraordinary things with tremendous clarity and decisiveness. You will find that you actually gain time and effectiveness by refraining from work for thirty-six hours.

Food Is Your Primary Energy Source

Watch your diet carefully. Discipline yourself to eat healthy, high-protein, low-carbohydrate foods. Eliminate the three white poisons—sugar, salt, and flour. During crunch time, discipline yourself not to eat bread, desserts, candy, soft drinks, or pasta. Instead, eat more fruits and vegetables and high-quality proteins.

Your brain is like a massive supercomputer. When you are working in your business, your brain consumes 80 percent of the energy used by your entire body. It is like an automobile engine with your foot on the accelerator and the car in neutral. During crunch time, brain functioning burns up an enormous amount of glucose, which leaves you tired out, distracted, irritable, and often unable to make good decisions. When you eat high-quality foods, especially first-class proteins such as fish, eggs, lean meat, and similar foods, your body converts this protein into the high-energy glucose that your brain needs to operate at peak performance.

Drink lots of water. You need eight full glasses per day. You can drink coffee, but in moderation. And don't drink soft drinks at all. They contain sugar, caffeine, and other substances that can give you emotional highs and lows. Take care of your body as if you were a prize athlete about to go into competition.

Get Lots of Exercise

Finally, to conserve energy and take excellent care of yourself, get 200 to 300 minutes of exercise each week, thirty to sixty minutes per day. You should exercise in chunks of thirty minutes or more, but you don't have to train for the Olympics. Just going for a vigorous walk around the block for a half-hour each evening will pump up your heart, improve your balance and coordination, relax and calm you, and give you a feeling of well-being. Sustained aerobic exercise of any kind, such as riding an exercise bike or a cross-country ski machine or playing any active sport, will dramatically improve your ability to think, function, and perform during crunch time.

When you exercise vigorously, your brain releases endorphins. These are often referred to as nature's "happy drug." When these endorphins hit your system, they give you an enhanced sense of well-being and exhilaration. You feel more positive, confident, and creative. Endorphins make you more personable and genial with other people. They lower your psychological "flashpoint" and allow you to remain calm and effective, even in the most stressful circumstances.

Start Your Day Right

Henry Ward Beecher once wrote, "The first hour is the rudder of the day." The way that you start your day sets the tone for everything that happens in the following hours. If you lay out your exercise clothes before you go to bed, and then get up and exercise immediately for thirty to sixty minutes, even if you just go for a brisk walk, you will be set up for the day. If you follow your exercise with a high-quality, high-protein breakfast, your brain will be supercharged and you will be ready, like a star athlete, to perform at your best.

Remember, nothing is more important than your *health*. Crunches will come and go, but your health is always with you. There is nothing that happens in the outside world that can justify sacrificing your long-term health and well-being. Your life is precious. Take good care of your health, especially during crunch time.

Crunch Point Actions

1.   Treat yourself like a prize athlete in training for Olympic competition; eat only those foods that are really good for you, such as lots of fruits and vegetables and lean-source protein, and drink plenty of water each day.

2.   Resolve to get at least thirty minutes of exercise each day, even if it is only a brisk walk in the morning or evening. This activity will lower your stress levels and help you to perform at your best mentally.

"Obstacles are necessary for success because victory comes only after many struggles and countless defeats. Each struggle, each defeat, sharpens your skills and strengths, your

men attributed their success in business to their habitual use of this greater mind. Many psychologists and mystics refer to it as the *superconscious* mind, or the *collective unconscious*. Ralph Waldo Emerson called it the *oversoul*.

If you are spiritually inclined, you will see this as the *God mind*, or the power of God, available to you and working through you, wherever you are and whenever you want. In the Book of Psalms, this power is referred to as "a very present help in trouble." It is always available, anywhere and anytime. You need only turn to it in any difficulty and this great power will become available to you.

Tap into the Unlimited Power

This power can solve any problem, resolve any difficulty, and give you the insights and ideas you need to surmount any obstacle. It is easy to contact. You can use meditation, contemplation, solitude, or prayer to make your connection with this power at any time, including this very moment.

The most powerful way to tune in to this greater mind is to develop an attitude of faith, an attitude of *calm, confident expectation* that all will be well. This mental attitude seems to be the catalyst that causes this greater mind to activate and go to work in your life.

When you turn to this great power, it will automatically and continuously solve every problem on the path to your goal, as long as your goal is clear. In times of turbulence and confusion—as in a crunch point—your long-term goals may be fuzzy and contradictory. For this reason, to tap into this great power, your goals should be, first of all, peace of mind, and second of all, a happy resolution to whatever challenges you are facing.

Trust in This Power

The calmer you are, the more rapidly this spiritual power works to solve your problems and get you out of the crunch. Sometimes this power works immediately. It is said that "God is ready the moment you are."

The wonderful thing about this power is that the greater *trust* you have in it, the more rapidly and predictably it works, sometimes in the most unexpected ways.

There is a story of a farm boy who was playing one day, walking on the top of the corrugated tin roof of a three-story barn. Suddenly he slipped, lost his balance, and began sliding toward the edge of the thirty-foot drop. Panicking, he cried out, "Please God, help me." Just at that moment, his pants caught on a nail and he stopped sliding toward the edge. He looked up and said, "Never mind, God, my pants are caught on a nail."

Keep Your Eyes Open

Many people are like that little boy. They pray for a resolution to their problem and when it comes, they fail to recognize its source. Once you "put in your order" for help in getting out of a crunch, you must remain open to all the little things that are happening around you. Your solution may come in the form of a phone call, a magazine or newspaper article, or a casual remark at an unexpected time. The rule is that "whatever you want, wants you." Remain alert and aware of all possibilities.

Talk to yourself positively to keep yourself in the right frame of mind. One of the things that I say over and over to myself is, "I believe in the perfect outcome of every situation in my life because God is in complete control."

One of my favorite passages from the Bible is, "The will of God for me is always good and perfect and acceptable." By repeating sentences like this, you attune yourself to this higher power and allow it to work through you and for you.

Seek the Valuable Lessons

This power brings you the lessons you need to achieve your goals and to be successful and happy in the future. You must recognize them as lessons when they occur. Your greatest blessings often come disguised as setbacks, problems, and temporary failures.

After twenty years of interviewing successful people, Napoleon Hill came to the conclusion that "within every problem or difficulty lies the seed of an equal or greater benefit or opportunity."

Whatever difficulty you are experiencing, look for the lesson that you are meant to learn from it. Sometimes, the lesson contains far greater value than the cost of the problem itself.

Practice Solitude

Throughout history, great men and women have been men and women of faith. It is said that a person becomes great when he begins to take time to spend quietly with himself.

The way that you tune into this higher power on a regular basis is by taking time off to sit in silence, to pray or meditate in complete *solitude*.

During this period of prayer or solitude, you simply let your mind relax. Don't worry or try to think about anything, especially your problem. One technique to help you achieve this calm mental state is for you to think about water while you are sitting quietly. Think about a deep pool of still water, or even better, sit and look at a swimming pool or lake. This activity seems to calm the mind at a deep level.

The practice of solitude requires a minimum of thirty minutes, and longer if possible. For the first twenty minutes that you spend in solitude, you will have an almost irresistible urge to get up or do something. Your mind may jump around from subject to subject. But you must remain still.

After twenty or twenty-five minutes, you will start to relax and your mind will become calm and clear, like a mountain lake.

Then, as you sit there quietly, allowing your mind to float freely, exactly the answer you need to your most pressing problem will arise in your consciousness. You will receive an insight or an inspiration to do something that will turn out, in retrospect, to be exactly the right thing for you to have done at that time.

Activate the Law of Attraction

Through the practice of prayer and contemplation, you activate the Law of Attraction. You turn your mind into a magnet that attracts ideas, people, information, and resources that help you to solve your problems and achieve your goals.

Each time you tap into this power, which is always available to you, it becomes easier to do so in the future; and it will work even more rapidly.

Prayer, meditation, and solitude are perhaps the most powerful of all methods you can use to get yourself out of any crunch in work or personal life. Take the time to connect with the higher power on a regular basis, and expect to see miracles unfold around you.

Crunch Point Actions

1. Resolve to practice solitude for a half-hour or more each day, either first thing in the morning, before you eat or drink anything, or at the end of the day. Be prepared for incredible ideas and insights.

2. Have faith. Be completely confident that there is a solution to your biggest problem and that it will appear in your life at exactly the right time for you.

"I know this world is ruled by infinite intelligence. Everything that surrounds us—everything that exists—proves that there are infinite laws behind it. There can be no denying this fact. It is mathematical in its precision."

—THOMAS EDISON

C H A P T E R   2 0

Character Is King

"Work joyfully and peacefully, knowing that right thoughts and right efforts will inevitably bring about right results."

—JAMES ALLEN

The only thing that is inevitable in the life of the leader, or in anyone's life, is the crisis. You will experience crunch points over and over again throughout your career. They seem to be a normal and natural part of being an adult in a fast-moving, highly competitive society. Reversals and disappointments are unpredictable and unavoidable.

Crunch time comes upon you when you least expect it, and in spite of all of your best efforts to avoid it. The only thing that you can do when you hit the wall is to respond to it effectively and well. This is the true test of character and leadership. Anyone can be positive, optimistic, honest, easygoing, relaxed, and personable when everything is going well. It takes no discipline, willpower, or character. But it is when everything is going *wrong,* when you are threatened with financial or personal loss and you are seemingly overwhelmed with difficulties, that you reveal your true inner strength.

Everyone Is Watching

During a crunch point, everyone is watching you. Everyone is especially sensitive to what you do and say. If you are the head of your family or the leader of your business, your emotions and behavior set the tone for everyone else. How you behave triggers similar behaviors and reactions in others.

In more than fifty years of research, Dr. Edward Banfield of Harvard University found that the key determinant of success, happiness, and character is a person's *time perspective*. This was defined as how far into the future you looked when you decided on your present actions.

Superior men and women have a long time perspective. They think and project weeks, months, and years into the future. They look at everything they do in the present as part of a process that can have significant consequences in the future.

Recognize Your Most Valuable Asset

In life and business, your most valuable asset is your reputation. Your reputation consists of what people think and say about you when you are not present. It is the overall assessment that people have of your qualities and your character.

The rule with regard to your reputation is that "everything counts!" Everything you do (or fail to do) adds to or detracts from your reputation. It helps you or hurts you. It builds up your reputation or tears it down.

In a crisis, when you hit crunch time, everything you do is exaggerated. Your behavior can have far greater impact on your reputation than the things that happen during normal times. It is during the crisis that you demonstrate who you really are, deep down inside.

Rise to the Challenges

Strong people rise to the challenges of life. Weak people come apart and behave poorly. Strong people take a deep breath and confront the crisis in a straightforward way. Weak people become upset and angry and lash out at the people around them.

In times of crisis, the people around you need you to be calm, firm, and steady. You must be like the captain at the helm of a ship in a storm. No matter what is happening around you, you need to be calm, relaxed, alert, and in complete control.

Superior people continually think about the effect of their words and actions on the people around them, especially when the people around them are nervous or afraid. During a crunch point, you must go out of your way to calm and reassure the people who look up to you.

Refuse to become angry or upset when things go wrong. Refuse to criticize, condemn, or complain. When you express negative emotions of any kind, it makes you look weak. Complaining and criticizing takes your power away and makes you less effective.

When you receive bad news, especially involving mistakes that other people have made, be kind, compassionate, and friendly. Resist the natural urge to accuse and blame people when they have done foolish things. Remind yourself that, this too shall pass.

Diffuse the Crisis

Abraham Lincoln was famous for diffusing crisis situations by telling a story or a joke with a point. Sometimes, you can take complete control of a situation by telling the other people a story about something similar that happened, and then reaffirming your confidence that there is always a solution to any problem.

One of the most important things you do in a crisis is to reaffirm your values, and the values of your organization. Tell yourself, and everyone around you, that no matter what the situation, you will always do the right thing. You will behave with honesty and integrity. You will treat people fairly. You will not compromise your values for anyone or anything.

The foundation of self-confidence is a *commitment to values*. Based on your values of integrity, truth, honesty, sincerity, and straightforward dealing, determine the very best way to handle the crisis. What should you do first? What should you do second? How should you talk to or treat other people involved?

Think About the Solution

A person of character gets everyone thinking in terms of solutions and what can be done to resolve the crisis. Think in terms of specific actions you can take, right now. Refuse to discuss or worry about a past event that cannot be changed. Instead, concentrate all your energies on what you can do in the moment to resolve the situation. Get everyone so busy working on the solution that no one has the time to worry about what has happened.

Pass the Test

In school, the only way that you can move up to higher grades is by passing the tests at your current level. From now on, whenever you have a difficulty of any kind, large or small, simply look at it as a test. Think of everything that happens to you in life, especially setbacks, obstacles, and disappointments, as a type of test. Resolve that no matter what the situation, you will pass the test and move onward and upward to the higher grades of life.

The reward for solving problems is that you get the opportunity to solve even bigger problems. The measure of a person can be determined by the size of the problems that are entrusted to that person. Never complain about a problem, difficulty, or crisis. Instead, look upon it as an opportunity to grow more surely toward the stars.

Stepping Stones vs. Stumbling Blocks

Crunch points are inevitable, unavoidable, and unpredictable. The way you behave in a crunch can build you up or tear you down. Your ability to handle a crisis effectively is the most identifiable characteristic of leadership. From now on, whenever you have a problem or difficulty of any kind, look upon it as a special opportunity that is sent to help you to become stronger and wiser, and to be more successful and influential in the future.

Finally, remember that the best time to deal with a crisis mentally is *before* it occurs. Resolve in advance that no matter what happens to you today or in the future, you will remain calm. You will not overreact. You will take a deep breath, get the facts, and assert control. Resolve in advance that you will behave as a leader, as a person of courage and confidence, of strength and character. Then, when the inevitable storm rolls over you, you will be mentally prepared to perform at your best.

Crunch Point Actions

1. Make a list of three to five qualities that you admire in others and that you want people to think you possess. What could you do to demonstrate that you already have these qualities?

2. Resolve in advance that no matter what happens, you will never compromise your values for any reason. You will always behave consistent with the very best that you know.

"No, there is no failure for the man who realizes his power, who never knows when he is beaten; there is no failure for the determined endeavor; the unconquerable will. There is no

failure for the man who gets up every time he falls, who
rebounds like a rubber ball, who persists when everyone else
gives up, who pushes on when everyone else turns back."

—ORISON SWETT MARDEN

Pull It All Together

"Life is a series of steps. Things are done gradually. Once in a while there is a giant step, but most of time we are taking small, seemingly insignificant steps on the stairway of life."

—RALPH RANSOM

There is no problem you cannot solve, no difficulty you cannot overcome, and no crisis that you cannot deal with when you use your incredible powers of mind and character. Remind yourself that all of life is a test of some kind, and you fail the test only if you give up.

Here are twenty-one things you can do to take complete charge of anything that happens to you in the challenging weeks and months ahead:

1. *Stay calm.* Take a deep breath and refuse to become upset or angry. Lower your emotional flashpoint by asking questions, listening carefully, and thinking only about possible solutions.

2. *Be confident in your abilities.* Remind yourself that you have successfully handled all kinds of difficulties in the past, and you can handle this problem as well. Determine the worst possible outcome, and then make sure it doesn't happen.

3. *Dare to go forward.* Unexpected reversals and setbacks often stun you into a form of paralysis, triggering the fight-or-flight reaction. Instead of giving in to these feelings, think of specific actions you can take immediately to remedy the situation.

4. *Get the facts.* Events are seldom as bad as they first appear. Take the time to find out exactly what has happened before you make a decision.

5. *Take control.* Accept 100 percent responsibility for dealing effectively with the problem or crisis. Refuse to make excuses or blame anyone else. Don't dwell on the past, which cannot be changed. Focus on what can be done in the future.

6. *Cut your losses.* Don't cry over spilled milk. Practice zero-based thinking and ask, "Knowing what I now know, is there anything that I wouldn't start up again, or get into, if I had to do it over?" Be prepared to walk away from a situation that cannot be saved.

7. *Manage the crisis.* This is the "testing time" that always comes to leaders, adults, and people in positions of responsibility. Take charge, make a plan, and get busy resolving the problem.

8. *Communicate constantly.* Tell everyone who is affected by the crisis exactly what is going on. Practice a "no surprises" policy. Keep people inside and outside of your organization informed, and ask for input and assistance.

9. *Identify your constraints.* Determine the most important goal or objective you could attain to get yourself out of

this crunch, and then identify your key constraint, the *limiting factor* that determines the speed at which you attain that goal. Focus on alleviating that single constraint.

10. *Unleash your creativity.* You are a potential genius; you can find a solution to any problem you face. Think on paper. Define your problem clearly, develop as many possible solutions as you can, and then take action.

11. *Focus on key result areas.* There are seldom more than five to seven key result areas in any job or company. These are the things that you absolutely, positively have to do well to succeed in your business and your job. What are yours? How could you improve in your weakest areas?

12. *Concentrate on priorities.* Apply the 80/20 rule to everything you do. Remember that 80 percent of results comes from 20 percent of activities. What can you—and only you—do that, if done well, will make a real difference? Determine the most valuable use of your time at every moment, and focus on doing that one thing immediately and well.

13. *Counterattack!* Once you have assessed the situation, gathered your information, and made your plans, it is time to go on the offensive. Think exclusively in terms of actions you can take immediately to solve the problem and get through the crunch. Take command.

14. *Generate cash flow.* Most business and personal crises involve money in some way. Cash flow is like blood to the brain of the enterprise. Your job is to focus single-mindedly on preserving the cash you have and generating more. Let nothing distract you from solving a cash flow problem.

15. *Care for your customers.* The purpose of a business is to create and keep enough customers to ensure the survival and success of the enterprise. When your business experiences a crunch point, you must make every effort to keep your customers buying and paying.

16. *Close more sales.* Money in your customers' pockets or bank accounts doesn't do you any good. You must aggressively ask your customers to buy and pay for your products and services so that you can get out of your cash crunch. Be determined and insistent.

17. *Keep things simple.* In a crunch or emergency, you may find yourself overwhelmed with too much going on and too many things to do. But there are only a few things that really matter in the big picture and you must discipline yourself to focus on only those activities. Decide upon those things that you are not going to do. This is the key to simplification.

18. *Conserve your energy.* Take excellent care of your physical health. Imagine that you are a champion athlete preparing continually for an important competition. Eat the right foods, get lots of rest, drink lots of water, and exercise thirty or more minutes each day so that you can always perform at your physical and mental best.

19. *Make your connection.* There is a powerful universal mind available to you that can solve any problem and enable you to achieve any goal. All great people place their faith in this higher power and trust it to guide and inspire them regularly, especially in crunch time. Take an hour in solitude and listen for the "still, small voice within." It will always bring you the answer you need at exactly the right time.

20. *Character is king.* You demonstrate your true character when you are under stress, when you face setbacks, reversals, and the unavoidable crises of adult life. Resolve in advance that you will rise to any challenge and that you will never compromise your integrity for any reason. Act as if everyone is watching, because they are.

21. *Resolve to persist until you succeed.* Your decision to never give up is the ultimate guarantor of your eventual suc-

cess. You will face a continual series of problems and difficulties throughout your life, but as you face up to and surmount each one, you become all you are capable of becoming, and you'll grow more surely toward the stars.

"Many men fail because they quit too soon. Men lose faith when the signs are against them. They do not have the courage to hold on, to keep fighting in spite of that which seems insurmountable. If more of us would strike out and attempt the 'impossible,' we very soon would find the truth of that old saying that nothing is impossible. Abolish fear, and you can accomplish anything you wish."

—DR. C. E. WELCH

Index

About the Author

Brian Tracy is one of America's top business speakers, a best-selling author, and one of the leading consultants and trainers on personal and professional development in the world today. He addresses 250,000 people each year on subjects ranging from Personal Success and Leadership to Managerial Effectiveness, Creativity, and Sales. He has written more than thirty books and has produced more than 300 audio and video learning programs. Much of Brian's work has been translated into other languages and is being used in thirty-five countries. He is coauthor, with Campbell Fraser, of the Advanced Coaching and Mentoring Program and the Coaching Excellence Program.

Brian has consulted with more than 1000 companies—IBM, McDonnell Douglas, and The Million Dollar Round Table among them—and has trained more than 2,000,000 people personally. His ideas are proven, practical, and fast-acting. His readers, seminar participants, and coaching clients learn a series of techniques and strategies that they can use immediately to get better results in their lives and careers.